HORROR MAN

To Bob Holness
in friendship
and with every good
wish always

Peter Underwood

Also by Peter Underwood:

A Gazetteer of British Ghosts

Into The Occult

HORROR MAN

The Life of
BORIS KARLOFF

*With an Appendix of the films
in which he appeared*

PETER UNDERWOOD

LESLIE FREWIN of LONDON

First published 1972 by
Leslie Frewin Publishers Limited,
Five Goodwin's Court,
Saint Martin's Lane, London WC2N 4LL

This book is set in Baskerville,
printed and bound in Great Britain by
R. J. Acford Ltd., Industrial Estate,
Chichester, Sussex

ISBN 85632 000 0

*To my brother JOHN
who took me to my first
Boris Karloff film more
years ago than either he
or I care to remember.*

Contents

CONTENTS

Author's Note

THE LIFE STORY of Boris Karloff is the history of the film-making industry: he saw it all from its hesitant beginnings, through its golden era and into its eclipse as the major entertainment medium. He moved with the evolution of motion pictures from those early days of silent, jerky pictures, when he appeared in dozens of now-forgotten dramas and serials, to the talkies, where he took over the grotesque and unusual roles after Lon Chaney died in 1930; through the great boom of the talking film in the 'thirties and 'forties and finally to colour and widescreen spectaculars. Karloff lived with it all. Beginning at the very bottom in the film industry, he rose to the very top – and between whiles he worked on stage, radio and, increasingly, as the 'one-eyed monster' grew to such proportions that it inevitably affected all our lives, in television.

In this work I have tried to show Karloff the man as well as Karloff the well-known actor, and the story, from his early days in Enfield, where I have sought out a number of people who still remember him, through his hard days in Canada and the States with touring stock-companies; his humble beginning in films and then his meteoric rise to stardom in *Frankenstein*; his hobbies and his private life. A success story in a million set against a background of films and filming in Hollywood and Britain.

In writing this book I am indebted to many people, particularly those private individuals whose personal memories I have called upon to recreate a picture of those far-off days before Karloff went to Canada in 1909. I have before me as I write a small photograph album containing a score or so of early photographs. On the first page is the inscription: *'Photographs by W H Pratt'* (Karloff's real name). One of the now faded 'snaps' shows 'Billy' sitting on a garden seat between two charming young ladies . . . and I gladly acknowledge that this is the kind of help that has enabled me to paint a picture of those early days. I am especially grateful to the family and those close to my subject for considerable cooperation and help, and I am under obligation to my good friend Richard M Howard for his interest and many helpful suggestions and for crowning his kindness by typing the final draft for this manuscript. All the illustrations in this volume are from my own collection, and in cases where specific acknowledgement has not been made I crave the indulgence of the individuals and companies concerned who will be well aware of the great difficulties of establishing the rights of such material.

Among printed sources I must particularly mention the late Jonah Maurice Ruddy's interview with Boris Karloff published in *Film Pictorial Annual 1938* and Samuel Grafton's article in the American edition of *Good Housekeeping* dated August 1955; both have been

AUTHOR'S NOTE

of considerable interest and help to me and, in common
with other published works that I have consulted, I have
acknowledged my sources in the appropriate places
throughout this work. I am also indebted to the many
individuals, obscure and well-known, who have gener-
ously and readily helped me with my enquiries and
assisted me with information which has helped me to
produce, I hope, a rounded and complete picture of my
subject.

Finally I must acknowledge the very real help and
specialised knowledge that I have obtained from the
British Museum and Westminster Reference Library;
and particularly from the British Film Institute where
Mr John Gillett, the Information Officer, and the
Reference Room staff have proved invaluable.

Writing this book has been a long but very pleasant
task; I had hoped that it might help to repay Boris
Karloff for all the pleasure his work in several spheres
has given me for almost as long as I can remember,
but he died before it was completed.

1971   PETER UNDERWOOD
                          Savage Club,
                          London, SW1

CHAPTER 1

Early Days

BORIS KARLOFF WAS born William Henry Pratt, but not at Dulwich as stated in all the reference books. His birth certificate shows that he was born on 23rd November 1887 at Camberwell, in south London, although the registration was at Dulwich, which probably accounts for the widespread mistake. The family of eight sons and one daughter had lived at Forest Hill Road, Dulwich, and it was there that the youngest member of the family and the subject of this work spent his early life.

In 1909 the scene is Chaseview, a comfortable, spacious house in Chase Green Avenue, Enfield: the home of Mr and Mrs Edward Pratt ... Because he was the youngest, William Henry was rather spoiled by his mother, Eliza Sara (Millard) Pratt, and yet this could no more than compensate for the fact that the boy grew up without knowing his father, Edward Pratt, of the Indian Salt Revenue Service, a patriotic man leading a romantic life in faraway lands. William never knew his father who died when he was a baby. On the death of his mother, when he was still young, he was largely brought up by his brothers and by his half-sister, Emma, who frequently used to 'pull "Billy" up'.

The Pratt family had moved to Enfield fifteen years before, in 1894, when young Billy was only seven. Thus, most of his childhood memories were to be of Enfield, in the valley of the Lea. The ancient market, dating from a charter granted by King Edward I, had not been closed many years when the Pratt family moved to Enfield – then with a population of 35,000 – and where Queen Elizabeth I had lived, both before and after her accession, at Elsynge Hall. Charles and Mary Lamb lived at Chase Side, between 1827 and 1833. It is only in comparatively recent years that the Borough has become a popular, residential suburb with a population of over 120,000. Significantly, the ancient market place is now a carpark. Miss Alice M Roe, a long-standing friend of the Pratt family, has told me of the many years that she knew Billy Pratt when he was a frequent visitor to their home, and she recalls the family living at The Willows, Slade Hill and later at Uplands Park. During my enquiries into the early life of '*W.H.P.*', as he liked to call himself in those days, and particularly in Enfield where he spent so much of his youth, I came across many examples of his unfailing kindness, his inherent thoughtfulness and of his unassuming generosity – although the family were far from well off, Mrs Evelyn Karloff reminded me in 1970, and young Billy Pratt would often walk miles to save a few coppers on bus or tram fares.

One afternoon he met by chance a young girlfriend on her way to school; a girl who had a great weakness for chocolate cream-buns. Billy persuaded her to stay away from school for the afternoon, by adding the inducement that if she would, he would buy her as many buns as she could eat! He was as good as his word, and

a very real and lasting memory for that girl is of having
tea with Billy and eating many, many chocolate cream-
buns! ... Another girl broke her tennis racket and
immediately and unhesitatingly Billy, also an enthusiastic
tennis player, gave the girl his own racket. Still another
young woman chanced to admire his tie-pin with its six
black Indian pearls and he immediately gave it to her.
As a girl has no use for a tie-pin her mother suggested
it be made into a dress ring. This was done and a very
charming ring it made: I had the opportunity of
admiring it, for the lady concerned still proudly possessed
the ring a few years ago.

Early in his life William Henry was to hear a lot about
actors and the stage, and by the time he was eight years
old one of his brothers was already on the stage, under
the name of George Marlowe. Among his successes,
George played with Fanny Ward at the old Strand
Theatre in *The Royal Divorce*. Later he gave up the
stage and went into partnership in the city with a
Swedish firm of paper-pulp merchants; yet still the
theatre interested him deeply and George Pratt found
an outlet for this interest in coaching budding actors at
amateur clubs and assisting generally at the Enfield
Amateur Dramatic Society. Each year, too, he was
responsible for putting on a show for the Enfield Cricket
Club.

Not that his brother's dramatic experiences really
encouraged young William, for, despite the fact that
George was an extraordinarily handsome man, he never
went very far on the stage and soon exchanged the
variety of stage life for the regularity of a city job. Still,
the impressionable young boy had smelt grease-paint and

he did his youthful best to emulate his brother. Each Christmas a play was performed at the church-hall of St Mary Magdelene for the parishioners' children, when the Band of Hope would put on an entertainment. Before long Billy Pratt became one of the regular actors. He gave the parts he played everything he had, acting lustily and loudly. In view of the roles that were later to make him famous it is interesting to recall that his very first part was the Demon King in *Cinderella*! Even for that first stage role he wore dark make-up and long, sinister robes Major Reeves is one person who still remembers William Pratt's stage *début*: the fearsome Demon King fluttering his black wings and uttering doleful words of doom in deep and mournful tones as he emerged from the trap-door. 'I am the Demon King . . .' 'I was about nine years old then,' Karloff told me in 1967, a mildly enthusiastic smile lighting up his avuncular features. 'I had no idea that I had struck oil!' Right then and there he knew acting was the only thing he really wanted to do for the rest of his life.

In another very early play he had the title role in *Mike the Gipsy*, also put on at St Mary's Parish Rooms. Alice Roe's sister, Edith, told me that he wanted her to play the heroine in that play, but she didn't do so in the end. Both the Misses Roe did a lot of amateur acting in their young days and were interested in the theatre all their lives. The Misses Roe had vivid and pleasant memories of 'quiet and unassuming and lovable' Billy Pratt. In 1965 they still treasured his music stool (his beautiful sister Julia, who married a clergyman, the Reverend A Donkin, was a wonderful pianist I was told). I was shown Billy's favourite garden seat under the mountain ash in that quiet, secluded garden in Enfield. Here the youthful Billy would sit on a summer's evening and once, sitting on this very seat with Alice on one side of him and Edith on the other, their mother, Mrs Roe, of whom Billy was very fond, took a delightful photograph which the sisters still possess . . . On a visit to the charming Misses Roe, I too, sat on the wooden seat with one sister on either side of me and for a moment the years slipped away and I think that all three of us felt that for a fleeting second a carefree Victorian summer evening returned to that peaceful spot so full of memories . . . I saw the outside step where in the evening Billy would sit beneath the hop, still growing against the wall and now spreading over the window . . . and his favourite corner seat in the drawing-room that he visited often and where, born actor that he was, he would tread heavily up and down the room, characteristically waving a finger and saying in an already mellowed voice: 'Do *you* know, Alice . . .' Miss Alice Roe was amused years later to see Billy in the film *Juggernaut* (where he 'did away' with a nurse *Roe!*) ask, in exactly the same manner as he walked across the set: 'Where *can* Nurse Roe be . . .'

It was from the house in Enfield that William Henry Pratt went, after attending Dr Starkey's School and the Grammar School, Enfield, to the ancient and revered Merchant Taylors' School, London, in 1899, where, we learn from the published *Register*, he stayed four years. In 1903 he left to attend Uppingham School, Rutland, where he remained until 1906. He detested both schools.

At Uppingham, the growing boy took a particular interest in sport and played all the usual games. He was an enthusiastic 'rabbit', he recalls, at cricket (later to become his great sporting interest) and rugger. His chief regret concerning his time at Uppingham was that he did not satisfy his love for music. He sang in the choir and got through two years of piano practice (under pressure!), yet he had this to say about that period of his life, over thirty years later: 'If only I had decided to work a little harder at music. I missed a great opportunity. The music master was a brilliant man. If any boy had music in his soul, he would have brought it out.' ... 'Yes,' he added when I reminded him of those early days, 'I made a great mistake there; although I had no particular aptitude for music, my mistake lay in not taking advantage of that man's great knowledge and patience.'

When he was nineteen, William matriculated and went to King's College, London, to complete his education and, following the wishes of his family, to read for the Consular Service. He succeeded in showing continual disregard for all forms of higher learning and he quietly pursued his passion for acting. His reports amply reflect the fact that he attended more plays than classes, for although he honestly believed that he did not possess the brain or the ability for so exacting an occupation, it was nevertheless taken for granted that he would go into some branch of the Civil Service. Beginning to be absorbed in the life of the theatre, he used to haunt the galleries of the London theatres of the day and for the rest of his life he remembered the wonderful trio: Beerbohm Tree, Lynn Harding and Constance Collier who hypnotised audiences at Her Majesty's Theatre and Lewis Walker and George Alexander in those great days of the theatre and the actor-manager.

As he grew up at Enfield, William saw less and less of his seven brothers, most of whom were connected with the Government Service in China or India, and who always seemed to be abroad following in the footsteps of their father in diplomatic careers. One brother was in the High Court of Bombay; another became Sir John Pratt, KBE, CMG (died 1970), an expert on China for the British Foreign Office and a lecturer at Cambridge. But from time to time there would be one or two of them at home, on leave, and they always tried to keep their younger brother in his place – each in turn taking the growing boy on one side with stern reproaches about his negligence in preparing for the serious life of the Consular Service; for although William Henry was never at any time keen on the idea of a life in the Diplomatic Corps and said so, again and again, it was the intention that he should follow the family tradition. As his brothers, one after the other, went into 'the Service', so one after the other they would come home to Enfield on leave and 'speak' to their younger brother. No sooner was he rid of one of them than another would come home and the pressure would begin again. 'There was always the general comment that I was going to the dogs,' he was to say in after years, 'and everyone thought they ought to do something about it!'

This brotherly benevolence in trying to reform the boy during the recurring periods of six months leave at a time, became a trifle annoying – yet, again, in later years William recognised that his brothers' intentions were sound, if unavailing. Looking back he gladly acknowledged that he owed much to their interest. 'They were all men of substance and standing,' he said, fondly, 'they impressed me with a sense of rightness and the need for doing the right thing.' In London in 1953 he described himself at this time as 'the black sheep of the family: a nuisance who didn't have any brains and didn't do any work and was always getting into trouble of one sort and another . . .'

His brother George had been dead for several years but the stage was now William's only interest. On every possible occasion he went to the theatre, read plays and did everything he could to satisfy his dramatic yearnings. Always keen on acting ('mad on acting' is the phrase I heard time and again in connexion with young Billy Pratt), he lost no opportunity of seeing all the worth-while productions in London. One lady friend told me of his taking her to see Henry Ainley with Lily Brayton in one of that renowned actor's famous performances, *As You Like It*, at His Majesty's Theatre (proprietor: Herbert Beerbohm Tree) in 1907, and I have handled a beautiful presentation copy of the play that he had purchased at the theatre and suitably inscribed and dated: *23.11.07 from W.H.P.* Back home at Enfield, the young woman discovered that she had left the book at the theatre and Billy lost no time in returning to London and to the theatre to retrieve the book for his friend who treasured it for over fifty years.

Always, his brother George's acting experience was held up to William by the older members of the family as the horrible example of what happened when one tried to get on the stage, and at length they announced a joint three-point declaration. One, he could not possibly succeed because he did not have George's looks or his talents; two, it would be complete folly for him to try to make the stage his lifework; three (finally and most important), *they would never countenance it!*

From my researches at Enfield and elsewhere, a picture has emerged of handsome William Pratt with his fine speaking voice, and I had related to me the shock, and something akin to shame, that greeted the news that he was going to London for an audition for the stage. 'How dreadful, we thought . . .' In fact, Mrs Evelyn Karloff has informed me that he never had a stage audition in England. The Pratts were a typical Victorian family, especially in their disapproval of the stage as a career. It is this atmosphere that we step into at Chaseview in 1909 . . . The whole family conjoined in badgering the twenty-two year old 'baby' of the family to understand that the dignity and stability of a consular career was vastly to be preferred to the insecurity and uncertainty of life on the stage. And in part they were right, for the tall, rather sombre youth did have a very thin time for nearly twenty years until, as he was wont to say, 'luck stepped in and smiled on me.'

But we have not yet arrived at that happy event . . . This is 1909 and William Henry Pratt feels that he must get right away and work things out for himself, on his own. He informs his family of his intention to leave home and is mildly surprised when no obstacles are placed in his way. 'Fortunately,' he said, 'none of my brothers were home at the actual time of my departure and I had no great difficulties to overcome.' He had occasion to go to a solicitor's office in Lincoln's Inn over a £100 legacy from his mother, and when the details were settled – there, in the solicitor's office – William tossed a sixpence, telling himself: 'heads – Canada;

tails – Australia.' It came down heads. With part of his legacy he bought a steamer ticket for Montreal.

During one of my visits to Enfield, I talked with a lady to whom Billy Pratt used to send dark-red roses; once, she told me, he sent thirty postcards to her in a single day! But there had been a little argument and Billy was emigrating. She remembered a poignant note to his departure for Canada. In the very room where the little drama had been enacted I heard how Billy had come that evening, the evening before he sailed, and asked for one of the dark-red roses from the bunch that he had brought. He was given one and took it away. It was the last time that lady, now older but still very charming, ever saw Billy Pratt in the flesh: the tall, handsome, serious, modest and endearing Billy with his heavy tread, and already slightly bowed legs . . . On 7th May 1909, he sailed from Liverpool for Canada, second class.

CHAPTER 2

Struggle for the Stage

IT WAS A quiet departure from his native shores for the
young man who regarded himself as the failure of the
family; yet, perhaps, it was fitting that he should slip
away almost unnoticed in the hustling crowd of eager
faces, lining the quay and hurrying hither and thither
about the ship. For never again would he leave England
without the fact being reported far and wide for all to
read . . . Canada, as always, was calling for immigrants
and there must have been many a man who kissed his
wife or sweetheart goodbye that dank, November day,
comforting her with promises of the Utopia ahead of
them one day on the other side of the Atlantic. A few
found it, but for many it remained forever beyond
their reach. How many hopeful, trusting partings took
place that day, only to end in despair and silence; how
many *au revoirs* proved to be goodbyes?

No such melancholy thoughts troubled the tall,
huddled figure who impatiently strode the deck. William
Henry Pratt, an unfamiliar, tight feeling in his throat,
was anxious to be under way now that he had taken
the irrevocable step. He was not to know that in the
years to come and before he would see his native land

25

again, the name that he would adopt was to become a household word throughout the world, nor that the fame of his portrayal of Mary Shelley's monster would add a new word to English dictionaries.

He was at last aboard ship, without the slightest presentiment of what the future held. Neither were his thoughts especially concerned with the future. He was thinking of the present. And that wistful young man, facing alone a new life in a new world, has recalled how he imagined at this poignant time the brotherly sighs of relief echoing around the various outposts of the then extensive and far-flung British Empire!

He had £150 in his pocket, and was happy in his choice, although he had no idea of what Canada was like. His plans were to learn farming in Ontario, where he had been told a job was waiting for him. Later on, he hoped to buy some virgin land and develop it by himself. Little did he think that before long he would be writing home frequently from Canada for money to live on. To a young man who had never before left the shelter and comfort of an established home and large family, it was all a fantastic and exciting adventure. He was to spend six weeks on a Caledonian farm with an Irish farmer, the son of a retired country gentleman, who had gone to Canada on a windjammer. Looking back many years later, he told me that it seemed to him incredible that he could have thought that such a brief apprenticeship would fit him for a life on the land; yet such is the boundless enthusiasm of youth that this was his intention.

When he eventually reached the farm in Ontario, William was told that there was no job. Furthermore no one there seemed to have heard of him! However, it was the busy season and they offered him a temporary job which, he was told, might last a few weeks. He took the job and stayed in Caledonia for six months. Then one day he set off for Banff. The rugged beauty and impressive grandeur of the Rockies appealed to him deeply, and indeed those early days in Canada always remained a vivid memory, although his life in England had been paradise compared with his life in Canada at this time. Banff itself he loved, but he soon discovered that the area, charming as it was, was of little use to him as a place to find work. Still wandering westwards, he had exactly a pound in his pocket when he arrived in the beautifully-situated city of Vancouver in 1910: still unsure of what he wanted to do. With high hopes, he set out to look for work in the city he always referred to as 'the metropolis of the west'.

Even in those days his first thought was the stage, but everywhere he called he was told there wasn't a hope in hell of any acting work! There was little enough doing in the theatre at that time in any case, and worried managers were not interested in young Englishmen with no experience. The dire necessity of eating caused him at length to look elsewhere for work; for any kind of work that would bring in some money to ease the craving hunger that was beginning to be with him almost constantly. He discovered that workmen were required to dig a new racetrack and lay a fairground. The pay was one-and-threepence an hour. He went along and was signed on.

On the first morning, William reported for work without having had any breakfast. He simply had no money to buy any. That first day seemed a very long one: ten hours of dreary pick and shovel work, and his hands were badly blistered long before it was over. By the end of the week his hands had become hard and insensible. For the first three days he lived on threepence a day, because the arrangement, made by an astute foreman, was that workmen should be paid on Saturdays. Thirty years later, William Henry Pratt still regarded the steak he bought at the end of that first week as the finest meal he had ever tasted. True enough it was a living, but it did not take him long to realise that such work as this was no fun. He had almost reached the point of throwing in his hand and setting off again to look for something better, when he chanced to run into a Dulwich school-friend of one of his brothers.

Hugh Arthur spotted him at the same time and recognised the likeness between the two brothers. There in the street they chatted about faraway England, and then for a few moments they discussed William's brother John, who was then in China. As the conversation turned on what William himself was doing, Hugh Arthur pointed out that there was currently a boom in land, and suggested William should become a real-estate salesman. Always ready to try his hand at something new, William listened and agreed to give it a try. Once he had started, he found that he was little better than a glorified office-boy, but nevertheless he began to make a little money and occasionally he would give Hugh a couple of pounds towards buying a plot of ground. Then he would have a thin time and need the money he had saved. Before long, William Pratt could see that things were not going to work out well and the lack of any immediate return proved to be too hard a deterrent to overcome.

Turning his back on the real estate market he took to shovelling coal and then, having obtained an introduction to the Works Superintendent of the British Columbia Railway, he got a job at two shillings an hour laying track with a pick and shovel. This time he found the manual labour less of a hardship, and talking to me about this period of his life many years later he said, philosophically, that it was remarkable how soon youth gets used to work, no matter how rigorous and demanding it might be.

Late in December 1910, William Henry had occasion to call at the Hotel Vancouver. As he passed through the lobby he noticed a man whose face he thought distinctly familiar. Upon enquiry he discovered that it was in fact his brother John, on his way home from China to London! John, familiar in his role of the elder brother, listened to William's plans and the account of his repeated attempts to get stage work of some kind. At the end of the evening, he sportingly loaned his young brother twenty pounds. This was enough to keep young William going for quite a while, and he was always grateful for this practical help at a very difficult time.

This financial backing, small as it was, gave the struggling would-be actor some independence and helped to boost his flagging confidence. For months on end he made repeated overtures to three Vancouver stock-companies. But there seemed not the slightest hope of becoming so much as an assistant to an assistant! He even went down to Seattle to see a theatrical agent he had heard of, introducing himself as an English actor (!) and spinning a yarn about his West End successes! 'He didn't believe a word of what I told him, of course,' William Henry Pratt added with a chuckle as he related this story when he was in London in 1953. 'But I had at least *seen* the plays I talked about!'

One evening, when in a despondent mood – and even then he read all the vacancy columns in stage journals – he happened to see an advertisement for an *experienced* character actor; it looked a perfect opening but his heart sank as he saw the job was with the Ray Brandon Players of Kamloops, some two hundred and fifty miles away. Nevertheless, he decided to apply for the job. Quickly he wrote out his application and made to sign it. As he was about to write his signature he suddenly stopped, and thought for a moment. Pratt didn't seem a particularly good stage name. He remembered a remote family name on his mother's side: Karloff. He searched his mind for an appropriate Christian name, and, 'out of the air', as he used to say, he thought of Boris and this seemed to fit as well as anything. Writing the name for the first time was, appropriately enough, the starting point of a new life for Boris Karloff, as he had named himself. And since he was afterwards always known by that name we, like him, will now drop his baptismal name and henceforth refer to him by his adopted pseudonym.

To his immense surprise a letter arrived within a few days (while Karloff was out with a survey team), inviting him to join the theatrical company at Kamloops at the princely sum of £6 a week. 'The company had a bad reputation and no one would join it,' Karloff said

30

modestly, 'that's why they sent for me.' To Kamloops he went, his determination diluted with trepidation, for this was to be his first professional stage work. He had no knowledge of such things as rehearsal routine, or make-up, or the foggiest idea of how to cope with stage direction – or other actors.

His first part was that of a man of sixty: Hoffman, the banker husband in a play called *The Devil* by Ferenc Molnar, one of the principal works of this brilliant playwright which showed the Devil as an engaging fellow who is a master of means to marital infidelity. At the end of the first performance the new, 'experienced' actor was slinking away to some dark corner when the manager approached him with a malevolent gleam in his eye. 'Karloff,' he said, 'You know darn well that you've never done stage work before. Still, you might make an actor and you can stay with us – at £4 a week.'

Karloff did stay with the company, for over a year, touring western Canada; and he quickly became popular as a villain. Then, early in 1912, the company was stranded in Regina, Saskatchewan. Everyone in the company without exception was absolutely broke. The situation looked bleak and the prospect dismal. 'Maybe the finger of Fate was pointing at me that day,' Karloff said, years later. 'For the very day after the manager announced our complete lack of funds and inability to proceed with the tour, the famous cyclone hit us: the only cyclone in the history of Canada!'

By next morning the whole world seemed to have blown away – show manager, week's salary, and half the town as well! But it was a case of an ill wind, because Karloff and his fellow actors all got work cleaning up the debris. And when the town was at last cleaned up, Karloff regretfully parted with the Ray Brandon Players and took a job loading luggage on the railway.

Before long he heard that a haulage concern, the Dominion Express Company, needed men and the rugged, husky out-of-work actor soon found that he had landed himself with yet another job. But always he could think of nothing but getting on the stage, and before long Lady Luck again stepped in. The haulage-company sent Karloff to the railway station to collect some crates of goods and as he crossed the track to the warehouse, someone threw an old copy of *The Billboard*, a theatrical journal, from the window of a passing train. Casually, Karloff picked up the magazine and glanced through it. His eyes lighted upon an announcement that the Harry St Clair Players, a repertory company up at Prince Albert, wanted a young leading-man. He hurried off a letter of application and received a reply a few days later asking him to join the company in Prince Albert, Saskatchewan.

The company, including Karloff, played in Prince Albert for about two years and thanks to Harry St Clair, himself an old actor, who held back a certain percentage of Karloff's salary each week, the struggling leading-man managed to save £150. When his savings reached this figure Karloff decided that he had enough money to keep him going for a while and feeling that he now had sufficient acting experience to enable him to do so, he decided to try one of the bigger theatrical centres. He chose Chicago and arrived there on 13th October 1914. In that black year, Karloff tried hard to enlist in the British Army but the man who had endured many hardships and had even slept out in the open on cold nights in Canada, was turned down because, they said, he had a heart murmur. (Yet it was bronchial trouble that finally finished him fifty-five years later in his beloved England.)

In the early days of the First World War there was a bad slump in the theatrical business and try as he would Karloff could get no engagements. During the course of his wanderings he went to the Brinkham Theatre in Minnesota but found things very dull, and he was glad to be able to return to Prince Albert and rejoin Harry St Clair.

'St Clair was absolutely honest,' Karloff once told Helen Ormbee of the *New York Herald Tribune*. 'If there was no money in the box-office the ghost didn't walk, but whenever business was good he paid what he owed us. In some towns we stayed a week, in others we settled down for a run. It was in Minot, North Dakota, in an upstairs "opera house" that we stayed fifty-three weeks, doing two new shows a week and I played 106 parts in all!'

It was hard work, but Karloff began to feel that he knew something about the job that he was determined to succeed at. As Samuel Grafton put it in his article in the American *Good Housekeeping*, August 1955:

> As important as the ability to act, in the old stock companies, was the ability to get along on almost no money. Karloff was a profound student on this subject. A stock-company actor had, for instance, to learn to fry an egg on the bottom of an electric iron, propped up on his hotel-room floor between

33

the bedpost and the Gideon Bible. (No butter was used, because that would have made the egg slide off; and one had to keep jiggling the iron.) Canned soup, always mulligatawny, because it had meat in it, was cooked in a dresser drawer over a canned-heat fire. New suits were selected from uncalled-for garments at cleaning establishments. Since the cast pressed their own clothes, a man's electric iron, which also served as his egg cooker, was his most precious possession, thoughtfully bought and fiercely guarded. 'If you were going to be in a small town for any length of time and needed a boarding house,' said Karloff, 'You enquired around as to where the local school-teachers stayed and asked for lodging there. You could be sure the place would be very cheap and very clean.' Karloff was entirely happy in stock; he loved to act. He had no notion that he was ever going to scare anybody, or become the face at the window for the majority of mankind . . .

'We all took turns at being stage-manager,' Karloff told me, 'and we never had a dress or prop rehearsal. We must have done some terrible acting, but let me say a word for the intelligence of our audiences. In towns where we did a different play each night we asked the audience to vote for the one they wanted us to repeat as our closing bill. You couldn't fool that public; it invariably put its finger on the best play. Today, when I hear people speak condescendingly of the sticks, I remember that.'

Looking back on those experiences a quarter of a

century later, Karloff felt that probably the finest experience one could get in the theatre in those days was to be with one of the repertory companies. Occasionally taking over as stage manager he played parts in *Paid in Full; Charley's Aunt; East Lynne; Way Down East; Bought and Paid For; Baby Mine; What Happened to Jones; Why Smith Left Home* – and many more. 'Good experience,' he commented in 1968, 'but no money!'

Happy as he was with Harry St Clair, Karloff realised that success would only come by playing in the large cities, so once more he went to Chicago. And once more he failed to find work there, but, quite by accident, he discovered that Billie Bennett's road-company was going on tour in *The Virginian* and Karloff managed to persuade them to take him with them. They toured Minnesota, Iowa, Kansas, Colorado and Nevada and finally arrived at Los Angeles in December 1917. It was a district of Los Angeles that later became synonymous with filmstars and film-making, and indeed became the heart of the American film industry; a district with the magic name of Hollywood.

CHAPTER 3

Stock-Companies and First Films

EARLY MOVIES WERE in full swing when Boris Karloff arrived in Los Angeles, but at that time he had no idea of going into films. All his strivings were still towards a stage career.

In Los Angeles *The Virginian* company disbanded. Then Karloff discovered that the San Pedro stock-company had a series of engagements in Southern California, and he managed to obtain a place with them and enjoyed his first wanderings through that part of the world. The tour lasted some six weeks. Afterwards, he managed to team up with yet another repertory company, the Maude Amber Players of Vallejo, and for a while things looked brighter. With them he toured right through the lovely San Joaquin valley and ended up at San Francisco.

So life went on and the years passed: one stock-company after another, up and down the west coast and occasionally as far east as Chicago; until a serious influenza epidemic temporarily ruined the theatrical business in the west. The stock-company he was with disbanded, and again Karloff was out of work. Once more, his tough, early training on the land and on the road stood him in good stead and for two months he managed to earn a living, working long hours each day piling sacks of flour in a storeroom and loading lorries, before finding more work with stock-companies.

His top salary on the stage had so far never been more than ten pounds a week. Still, somehow, he managed to keep intact a tiny capital of twelve pounds, which provided him with a little security and enabled him occasionally to venture afield in search of more experience. While playing with the Lawrence Company in San Francisco he heard of a chance to get into a vaudeville act at San José run by an old friend, Alfred Aldrich. Karloff went down to see about it, buying a ride on the deck of a lumber steamer. He got the booking at San José, but as it did not last very long Aldrich went to Los Angeles, hoping to get a booking for the act there. But he was unsuccessful and the vaudeville act broke up. Knowing of his friend's failure to find a booking for the act, Karloff was amazed to get a letter from Aldrich asking him to go to what was, even then, the largest city in California. And wondering what it was all about, join him Karloff did.

In Los Angeles Aldrich talked to him about the up-and-coming film industry, and showed the faith he had in Karloff's future by loaning him sufficient money for food and lodging until he could make the rounds of what was, now, the only remaining acting outlet: the film studios.

Eventually, perseverance won through and at long last he obtained a day's work in a crowd scene, making his first appearance before a film camera. The title of that first film vanished from Karloff's memory, but he seemed to recall being assigned to be a member of a mob in a picture that was directed by Frank Borzage – later to become famous for his *A Farewell to Arms* (1932); *Little Man, What Now?* (1934); *Three Comrades* (1938) – at Universal City. Frank Borzage, who died in Hollywood on 20th June 1962, was the first film director to win an Academy Award; this was for *Seventh Heaven*, in which Janet Gaynor, one of the many stars he 'discovered', was named best actress in 1928.

Looking back on those very early days, Karloff said that no one thought anything at all about his acting and, similarly, he didn't think much of his prospects in pictures. Indeed, this general apathy seemed to be borne out by his unsuccessful attempts to follow up his initiation into films. All his attempts failed and at first that single day's work was all that he managed to obtain . . . Then, at last, he appeared in a couple of serials, but he'd discovered film acting to be a precarious occupation, and after a few months he gave up calling at the studio casting-offices, and went to San Francisco where he joined the Bob Lawrence Company at the Majestic Theatre for a three-months' season.

Meanwhile, Alfred Aldrich had remained in Los Angeles and while there he was good enough to scout around, looking for possible opportunities for his friend. His reports grew more hopeful and on returning to Los Angeles, Karloff was introduced by Aldrich to Al Mac-Quarrie, a film agent. MacQuarrie found Karloff a few day's work as a 'guinea extra' in a Douglas Fairbanks picture, *His Majesty, the American*. Karloff played a suave, Mexican soldier, and in later years used to refer to this as his first film part.

In those days the film magnates did not wax enthusiastic about Karloff's particular type, but when the work on the Fairbanks film was over, Karloff thought that he might as well make the rounds of all the agencies in Los Angeles. Late one afternoon, he entered the office of Mabel Condon. She saw him and was at once enthusiastic. Thanks to her good offices he obtained some small 'bit parts' and later larger parts in independent film productions.

After a small part in a Jesse Hampton picture starring William Desmond and Blanche Sweet, Karloff obtained his first real consignment in *The Deadlier Sex*, also with Blanche Sweet. Although rewarded with a more substantial role, his portrayal of a French-Canadian trapper instantly 'typed' him; as his singular portrayal of the Frankenstein monster was to do again years later in a more sombre role.

Karloff played in six or seven pictures as a French-Canadian trapper, spending three years in the film studio version of the North backwoods, and his pay rose to the dizzy heights of £50 a week. Working in several pictures had encouraged Karloff to forget the stage for a while, and he decided to remain and work in films for as long as he could . . . He sent home photographs of himself as a 'cowboy', Miss Alice Roe has told me, and she would look at the photographs and wonder whether she would ever see 'Billy' again. She never did.

Then suddenly, in 1923, the appeal of the North Woodsman pictures declined and the bottom fell out of Karloff's world; he made only one picture that year. Even in those days, there was a typing system and, because of his portrayals of French-Canadian trappers

39

and similar roles, and, perhaps, particularly because of his work in Richard Walter Tully's *Omar, the Tentmaker* in which he was quite prominently featured, nobody dreamt of hiring him to play anything else. Starring Guy Bates Post, *Omar, the Tentmaker* was an ambitious AFN film, released in 1922, and noted for its remarkable and beautiful settings. Unfortunately, the two-generation love story set in the days of Omar Khayyám had a 'scenario that was disappointingly cold and the continuity was ragged' – even for those days; while 'scenes of detail', complained a magazine, 'like shots of the potter's wheel, are interesting, but they slow down action and distract attention from the story.' And again: 'This is beauty, but not drama', and 'it is a pity that such surpassing artistry of settings should be wedded to such a dramatic triviality'. The acting however was 'good', reported the same periodical, and the photography 'excellent'. Viewed in retrospect, *Omar, The Tentmaker* was an inspiring picture, which attempted to portray the emotional atmosphere as well as the physical surroundings of the period. It particularly well portrayed the luxury in which the dissolute and half-witted Sultan reigned.

Out of work again, Karloff could have gone back into the 'extra' ranks, but he knew that once back there it would be more difficult than ever to emerge. He had seen it happen to other men, and he knew some who remained extras for the rest of their lives. It was difficult to say 'No' when he got a call for mob scenes and had not had a job for some time and meals were not too frequent, but he was strong minded and believed that once one had risen to the status of a 'bit player', one couldn't go back to being an extra – not in Hollywood – without being considered 'through'. At this time there was an almost insurmountable division in the motion picture business between those actors who made their wages as 'bodies' or atmosphere players (known outside Hollywood as 'extras') and the 'principals' who had speaking roles. Working as an atmosphere player was by no means a road to stardom, as Beth Day points out in her *This Was Hollywood* (1960); for, as a general rule, atmosphere players were not actors at all, since their kind of work consisted principally of 'standing and smoking' all day for a few seconds work before the cameras – and then the cameras were not aimed at them but at the principals who appeared in the scene. It was not the sort of work that appealed to people with any ambition. It was in fact the 'road to nowhere'. There was no chance of advancement . . . In those days an extra player could appear regularly in picture after picture for many years and still draw the same salary that he had started with; now, of course, in these enlightened days, union rules decree otherwise. In view of his resolution, Karloff tried to get back into stock, but he discovered that there were no stock-theatres any more. Movie competition had made itself felt, and a chapter in American show business had ended.

During those early days, Karloff saw another side of the film industry from the one featured in newspapers and magazines: the struggles of hundreds of ambitious youngsters who sometimes succeeded, but who all too often found no outlet for their talents. One of the stars he met during those lean times was the kindly and much-loved Lon Chaney, a master of grotesque and macabre make-ups. Many of these were created by Chaney personally (union rules now forbid actors creating or applying their own make-up); and among his masterpieces are the disguises for *The Hunchback of Notre Dame* (1923), one of the most ambitious undertakings of Carl Laemmle's Universal Pictures, and *Phantom of the Opera* (Universal, 1925). In the latter film, Chaney played his classic role of the maniac who abducted a singer from the Paris Opera and, after a chase through the cellars and sewers of Paris, met his death in the Seine. In later years, Karloff was sometimes acclaimed as a successor to Lon Chaney, but he disliked this and would shake his head and say: 'There was only one Lon Chaney.'

'I used to go to the Legion Stadium for the fights,' Karloff explained when speaking of Chaney, who died in 1930, 'and since I often lacked sufficient funds to go inside, I would stand outside and watch the more fortunate people enter. Chaney never missed a boxing bout and he always spoke to me pleasantly as he passed – we had met once at that time, on a movie set . . .

'One day after work, as I walked through the studio gates and set off home, I heard a big car honking behind me. I thought the driver wanted me to get out of the way. I had only fifteen cents in my pocket, but I had plenty of pride and I resented the honking. I slowed down and walked calmly ahead . . .

'The car slowed down too and a voice said: "Don't you recognise old friends, Boris?" . . .

'I looked inside the car and saw Lon Chaney smiling at me. He invited me to ride with him and for more than an hour he talked to me of the picture industry and asked me about my ambitions . . .

'That talk with Lon gave me courage to keep trying in later years when the going was far from easy,' said Karloff, with sincerity, 'one of the things Lon said was: "If you're going to act – you're going to act. Even if you have to starve, never give up. It's the only way".'

'Yes, there will only be one Lon Chaney,' affirmed Karloff, 'because he understood so well the souls of afflicted people. On that fateful afternoon he told me how he had suffered because his mother and father were deaf-mutes. None of us can do what Chaney did, because none of us feel it just as he did. He said too, "the secret of success in Hollywood lies in being different from anyone else. Find something no one else can or will do – and they'll begin to take notice of you. Hollywood is full of competent actors. What the screen needs is individuality!" '

Karloff was never to forget the kindness shown to him or the advice given to him that day by the great Lon Chaney, who incidentally, died as the result of something almost as strange, in a different way, as the grotesque roles he so often played. In more recent years feathers, salt and Polystyrene have been used to simulate snow, and, in *Oh! What a Lovely War* (1969), a form of chemical foam was used most effectively in the battlefield-fraternising scene, but years ago they used cornflakes; and in one of his last pictures Chaney was working in a snow scene and some of the dry cereal flakes lodged in his throat and caused an infection which eventually developed into a throat complaint which proved fatal.

43

Chaney, as Bosley Crowther recounts in *The Lion's Share* (1957), was a strange, ambiguous fellow who started his movie career in 1913 and learned his business in more than a hundred, assorted films. His *forte* was unusual make-up and he will always be associated with such roles as the fake cripple, Frog, in George Loane Tucker's historic *The Miracle Man*; the blind sailor, Pew, and a pirate in *Treasure Island*; a non-racial Fagin in the Jackie Coogan version of *Oliver Twist*; the mad and mis-shapen bellringer in *The Hunchback of Notre Dame*; the mad scientist in *The Monster*; the pock-marked Ricardo in Joseph Conrad's *Victory*; the insane waxworks curator in *While Paris Sleeps*; the crippled clergyman who lapsed into a Cockney thief in *The Blackbird*; the felon with a sickeningly-glaring dead eye in *The Road to Mandalay*; the armless knife-thrower in *The Unknown*; the crippled and sadistic magician of *West of Zanzibar*; the dual role of a Scotland Yard detective and a human vampire of exceptionally horrible appearance in *London After Midnight* (1927); and what was perhaps his greatest success, the 1925 version of *The Unholy Three*. Voted one of the best films of the year and grossing over $2,000,000, this film was full of surprising twists, and saw Chaney as the crooked ventriloquist who committed his crimes disguised as a sweet, old lady, with a dwarf disguised as a baby in his arms.

Chaney himself, like Karloff, was an amazingly gentle and self-effacing man, devoted to his profession and stubbornly shunning the Hollywood limelight. For his role in *London After Midnight*, Chaney had a set of thin wires in his eye sockets which he screwed up to cause his eyes to bulge. 'Unless I suffer,' Chaney used to say, 'how can I get people to believe me?' The same year he acted an armless, gypsy knife-thrower in *The Unknown* and to make the role truly realistic, Chaney invented a strait-jacket that pressed his arms so tightly against his body that he appeared to be completely armless. He knew that this would stop the circulation, and was warned that serious injury could result. Chaney ignored the advice, and the excess blood flowed into his legs and burst blood vessels there. In *Phantom of the Opera*, he inserted a painful device into his nose that widened the nostrils and put celluloid discs in his cheeks to push out the cheekbones, resulting in a skull-like appearance.

In 1930, Irving Thalberg and Chaney agreed that the silent star should make his belated *début* in talking pictures with a remake of *The Unholy Three*. Again, in the role of the ventriloquist-crook, Chaney projected with ease the totally differing voices of the dummy, the little, old lady, the midget masquerading as a baby and a parrot as well as using his own voice. But this success proved to be a swan-song for Lon Chaney. Already he was mortally ill. After his last day on the set he suggested the taking of a photograph of the entire company. The photograph was duly taken, the stage-crew happily rubbing shoulders with the star. Then Chaney shook hands with everyone and departed, never to return. He died on 26th August 1930, at the age of forty-four. 'Chaney was the king of the lot,' Karloff said to me in 1968, talking about horror actors. 'I only met him a couple of times when I was a struggling actor, but Chaney was undoubtedly a great, great man.'

45

CHAPTER 4

The Films Take Over

So BORIS KARLOFF in 1923 was broke. He tried desperately to find work with stock-companies, but there was no stage work to be found. Reluctantly he turned from the stage and began to look elsewhere. But he could find nothing. Then, one day he heard there was a lorry-driving job going with a concrete and cement firm in Los Angeles. He had never driven a car, let alone a lorry, but now he decided was the time to learn – quickly.

He spent the best part of the next day, a Sunday, with a friend who taught him the rudiments of driving, and the following day he applied for the lorry-driving job. He got it. Then he found that it meant driving a seventeen-ton truck!

'After,' as he put it, 'learning the idiosyncrasies and whimsicalities' of his new job he was sent out on an urgent delivery with three-hundred casks of cement. These had to be carried from the warehouse to his lorry, driven about twenty-seven miles and then unloaded. For this he received one pound a day. 'It wasn't really so bad,' he said, twenty-five years later, 'but I was a little older and for the first few days I ached in every muscle.' When the weather was wet the cement became staggeringly heavy and Mrs Karloff has said that there is little doubt that this was the beginning of her husband's back trouble, which he suffered from on and off for the rest of his life.

However the job had its compensations. Karloff got on well with the foreman, Charlie Curtis, a kindly man who listened to the young lorry-driver's plans for an acting career and arranged matters so that Karloff could take an occasional day off work to act in pictures and, at the same time, get a little relaxation. He obtained a fairly good part in *Dynamite Dan* and a fatter one, a few months later, in *Parisian Nights*, where he played a sadistic, Parisian *apache*. He always remembered this role and remained grateful to the director, Alfred Santell, and his assistant, Robert Florey. Many years later, Florey directed Karloff in the very successful television-film *The Incredible Doktor Markesan*.

It was really through Robert Florey, who was later to become a director at Universal, that Karloff had landed the role in *Parisian Nights*, an Elaine Hammerstein film, made at the old FBO studios. Karloff was tremendously grateful. 'People were very kind,' he told me in 1968, speaking of this period of his life, 'but I think they always have been to me.'

Things carried on this way for over a year. He acted in such films as *Prairie Wife*, *Lady Robin Hood* and *Forbidden Cargo*, where he appeared as a mate on Evelyn Brent's rum-running ship, playing in character and in one scene preparing to pour molten lead into the eyes of the hero . . . Then Karloff had the opportunity of going to San Francisco, on location, and appearing in *Never the Twain Shall Meet*, starring Bert Lytell. He decided to take the chance, but discovered that he couldn't have his cake and eat it, too, and this stay on location cost him his job handling cement. 'So,' as he used to put it, 'I just had to stay in pictures.'

During the next few years, Karloff worked briefly for First National in *The Greater Glory* and *The Love Mart*; for FBO in *Her Honor, the Governor*, *Flaming Fury* and *Tarzan and the Golden Lion*, a silent serial based on Edgar Rice Burroughs's book of the same name; for Paramount in *Eagle of the Sea*, *Old Ironsides*, *Let it Rain* and *Soft Cushions*; for Gotham in *The Golden Web*; for Chadwick in *The Bells*. And a couple of times, in *The Man in the Saddle* and *Burning the Wind*, at Universal City with its open-sided trams for transportation along the miles of concrete streets. He played, too, in *Two Arabian Knights* for United Artists-Howard Hughes – described as 'an excellent comedy' by Paul Rotha in *The Film Till Now* (1949). However, the stage still enthralled Karloff, the dedicated actor, and he was sincerely grateful when the brilliant English actor and producer Reginald Pole offered him a good part in *The Idiot*. 'Pole must have had astounding faith in my acting ability,' recalled Karloff, 'for I hadn't appeared in a stage role in something like seven years!'

It is interesting to recollect that about this time, 1926, the Central Casting Bureau was established by film producers as a clearinghouse for the convenience of actors, so that they could contact a central office for film work instead of making the rounds of the far-flung studios. In the middle 'thirties, recalls Beth Day in *This Was Hollywood* (1960), there were 20,000 people registered at the Bureau. In 1950 there were still 7,000 wouldbe actors registered for the three hundred jobs available each day. Then the Central Casting office succeeded in reducing the figure to the region of 3,000, by discouraging young people from remaining in the film business. These figures may well be sobering ones for the starry-eyed youngsters who envied their friends and indeed anyone who was 'in films.'

In *The Bells*, the screen version of Henry Irving's stage success, Karloff had a role of some consequence, playing the sinister mesmerist, with Lionel Barrymore as the conscience-ridden murderer. It was Lionel Barrymore ('a great man,' said Karloff, 'a much better actor than his brother John') who sketched out the idea for Karloff's weird, almost Caligari-like, make-up for his part in the film. Soon more acting opportunities came his way in Los Angeles, and in 1928, at the old Egan Theatre, he obtained the important part of Artem Tiapkin in *Window Panes* by O Printzlace.

The years passed; bit parts in films like *Little Wild Girl*; *The Devil's Chaplain*; *Phantoms of the North*; *Two Sisters*, fluctuated with such stage appearances as Kregg in C De Vonde and K Gordon's *Kongo* at The Capitol Theatre, San Francisco. But intermingled there were still periods when he was 'on the corner'—which is actors' talk for being out of work.

Then he made his first sound film, *The Unholy Night* (MGM, 1929), which Lionel Barrymore directed. Karloff used to refer to this film as *The Green Ghost*, the title under which the film was shot. He followed this by playing a penal colony guard in *The Bad One* (UA – Schenck, 1930); a clip from this film, showing a tall, lean Karloff, is included in *Days of Thrills and*

49

Laughter, 'a star-packed pageant of comedy and suspense from the golden age of films': produced and directed by Robert Youngson, this was shown on BBC television on 13th June 1968. Next, Karloff appeared on the screen as a villainous halfbreed in *The Sea Bat* (MGM, 1930); then as a bandit in a Tom Santschi Western, *The Utah Kid* (Tiffany, 1930), and as a corpse in *Mothers Cry* (Warner Brothers, 1930) . . . And then a day of destiny dawned for Boris Karloff.

He lived at this time in a little frame-house at the top of Laurel Canyon and he had a broken-down, old car in which he would roll down into Hollywood a couple of days a week to see a theatrical agent. On this particular day the agent was out, but Karloff was told that he would be back in an hour's time. He decided to hang about. He would have liked a cup of coffee but couldn't spare the money; he didn't feel like taking the traditional stroll along Hollywood Boulevard, for that would have meant seeing other out-of-work actors like himself. He couldn't go to his club, The Masquers, because his club subscription was long overdue . . . Odd, to look back and think that had he had the money to spare for a cup of coffee that day, the whole course of his life would probably have been different.

He decided at length to look in at the Actors' Equity office to see whether there were any letters for him. It was one of the things an actor did. Karloff had been doing it for years; there had never been anything for him. 'I never wrote home in those days,' Karloff explained to me, 'I had nothing to tell them except that I was broke.' But as Karloff climbed the stairs to the Actors' Equity office that afternoon, just to get off the streets for a few minutes, Lady Luck again stepped in . . .

There were no letters for him, but as he turned away from the desk the girl asked him whether he was working. When he said 'No', she suggested he go downtown, to the Belasco Theatre where they were casting a play: Flavin's *The Criminal Code*. Karloff knew that this play had run in New York and although they were now only casting the smaller parts, it would be a wonderful opportunity for him: and so indeed it turned out to be.

He hopped on to a street car, which could go faster than his jalopy, and as he used to put it, he was 'lucky.' He got the part of the killer of the piece, a minor role but brilliantly effective; that of a jail trusty who kills a 'stool-pigeon' or decoy. He seized the opportunity with both hands and really made something of the character. Unlike many actors who never got beyond supporting roles, Karloff possessed real acting ability and in this play it really shone through. The play was a success and ran for nine weeks in San Francisco and afterwards moved to Los Angeles, a shop window for actors; and when Columbia decided to make the play into a film starring Walter Huston, Karloff played his stage part of Galloway in the highly successful film. Yet even in this early film, Karloff had ugly, cropped hair and a sinister make-up!

Writing in *Film Weekly*, 18th April 1936, Karloff pointed out that the most difficult thing to realise about thrillers, as distinct from horror stories, is that the actor has to leave most of the hair-raising scenes to the imagination of the audience; he cites *The Criminal Code*, which he calls, 'the first talkie I made that really meant anything.' 'I had done this as a stage-play.' he goes on. 'The highspot was a prison scene in which I had to come on and kill a "stool-pigeon." It was a gripping scene, and you could have heard a pin drop in the theatre. Yet it required no acting. The stool-pigeon was on first. He had his back to the audience. Then I came on. As I walked across the stage I was staring at the stool-pigeon. The audience couldn't see my face fully. Then I turned and had my back to them as well. There was a moment of deathly silence, then the stool-pigeon turned. Before he could do a thing I had plunged a knife into him. He flopped to the floor. The audience still couldn't see my face. But they were imagining the most terrifying expressions on it – far more spine-chilling expressions than I could possibly have achieved. I had simply provided the frame; they had filled in the picture. When we came to make the talkie, the director Howard Hawks, asked me how that scene had been played on the stage. I told him and persuaded him to film it in exactly the same way. He wanted to take one or two close-ups of me as well, but I talked him out of the idea. I knew that a single shot showing my face would have spoilt the effect. Imagination alone provided those thrills. Imagination is the quality most needed in screen thrillers . . .' A clip from *The Criminal Code* was included in Karloff's last American film: *Targets* (1968/9).

After *The Criminal Code* (which featured Regis Toomey and Sue Carol, later Mrs Alan Ladd), film producers and directors seemed to notice Karloff; he began to find more regular work and supporting roles in films, some of them very good ones. Up to now, he had played 'heavies' mostly, appearing in lots of 'Backwoods' stories and five serials. Slowly he graduated to better roles and better films and, as the studios began to make full use of his talents, work came along fairly steadily. Outstanding during this period were *Cracked Nuts* with Bert Wheeler and Robert Woolsey; *Young Donovan's Kid* and *The Public Defender* with Richard Dix; *The Mad Genius* with John Barrymore; *I Like Your Nerve* with Douglas Fairbanks Jnr, and *Smart Money* and *Five Star Final* with Edward G Robinson. Karloff gave a particularly fine performance as a dope-peddler trying to 'hook' Jackie Coogan in *Young Donovan's Kid*.

A few months before Mervyn LeRoy chose Karloff for the double-faced reporter in *Five Star Final*, he was called in for an interview by Michael Curtiz who, on seeing Karloff, hesitated, but at length said: 'Well, I've called you over, so I suppose I shall have to use you.' Karloff didn't understand but he got the role of a Russian in *The Mad Genius*, the picture that Curtiz was currently directing for Warners.

The Mad Genius (released in 1931) was a sequel to Warner Brothers' first talkie adaptation of George du Maurier's *Trilby*, which they fittingly entitled *Svengali*, with John Barrymore in the title role of the sinister mountebank, hypnotist and musical genius. Barrymore brought pathos to his role in *The Mad Genius*, and there is a memorable scene where he attempts to seduce the hypnotised girl (Marian Marsh), only to recoil in self-disgust. The club-foot Barrymore with the soul of a ballet dancer finds his ideal prodigy in an orphaned child whom he nourishes to manhood (Donald Cook), and then loses to the young ballerina (Marian Marsh). The final scene depicts Barrymore's lifeless body dangling from an idol on stage during the performance of his ballet masterpiece.

Only years later when working on *The Walking Dead* in 1935, did Karloff learn the reason for Curtiz's momentary reluctance to put him in *The Mad Genius*. Michael Curtiz himself reminded Karloff of the incident. 'The reason I called you in,' he explained, 'was because I thought you actually were a Russian. Your name certainly sounded Russian! When you came in you seemed so anxious to get the job that I decided to let you have it!'

George E Stone, an old friend of Karloff's, who was himself in *Five Star Final*, had a lot to do with the keen, young actor getting a fairly important role in the film. Stone worked really hard for Karloff, talking to everyone about him and making sure that the producers could not miss knowing about the rising actor. Mervyn LeRoy had already been impressed with Karloff's work in *The Mad Genius*, but even so, Karloff always felt that LeRoy had great courage to give him the role of the religious, effeminate, newspaperman in a typical Edward G Robinson picture, and there is little doubt that the success he made of that role, and his work as a gangster in another newspaper story, *Graft*, greatly influenced Universal when they were looking for someone to take the part of the monster in *Frankenstein*, when that production was ready for filming.

It has been said that each time Universal have found themselves in financial difficulties over the years, they have resorted to horror films. Certainly they first turned the tide when things looked black with Lon Chaney's chillers, and after Chaney died the studio set about establishing a new horror star and settled on Boris Karloff, typing him for life when they cast him as Frankenstein's monster.

CHAPTER 5

Frankenstein

THROUGHOUT HIS LONG life, Karloff was asked many times: 'What's the best horror picture you ever made?'. His reply was always the same: 'Without a doubt, the original *Frankenstein*.'

It is interesting to consider whether Mary Shelley, wife of poet Percy Bysshe Shelley, would ever have written *Frankenstein* without the influence of her husband's genius. As one authority has put it: 'Nothing but an absolute magnetising of her brain by Shelley's can account for her having risen so far above her usual self as in *Frankenstein*.' Her other books are unremarkable, with the possible exception of *The Last Man*, a subject fit to range with *Frankenstein*, but it seems to be only half realized.

It was in 1816 that the Shelleys visited Switzerland and became neighbours of Lord Byron. The first time that Mary Shelley met Byron was at an hotel at Secheron, as Eileen Bigland relates in her biography, *Mary Shelley* (Cassell, 1959). As she and Shelley sat in the garden before dinner, she was 'surprised to see a slim figure in a dark green jacket and nankeen trousers approaching them. He walked with a curious half glide, half limp and was accompanied by a dark and handsome young man whom he introduced as his medical attendant, Dr Polidori . . . Mary especially admired his head, with its clear-cut features and long, waving, auburn hair, and was intrigued by the many gestures he made with his plump, white, beringed hands, which were, alas, marred by sadly bitten nails.'

Through the months that followed young Dr Polidori's behaviour grew more and more eccentric. The son of an English mother and a Tuscan father, he had studied medicine at Edinburgh and was only twenty years old when Byron engaged him. Unbalanced at the best of times, he developed an exaggerated idea of his own importance when John Murray offered him five hundred pounds for an account of his travel experiences with the poet. He was easily upset by the way in which both Shelley and Byron, whose intellects were far above Polidori's, ignored him during their long talks and he was soon subject to moods of black despair. Byron once found him about to swallow a dose of poison. This incident alarmed Mary Shelley and her husband who, with justification, felt that Byron's own life might not be safe while he was in the care of such a medical attendant. In fact some years later Polidori succeeded in committing suicide.

But, as Eileen Bigland points out, Polidori did make a contribution to the long evenings spent at Byron's villa during that wet, uncongenial summer, 'for he encouraged the company to discuss magic, superstition and all manner of supernatural subjects. One night they read aloud from *Fantasmagoriana*, a collection of German ghost stories.' And this macabre topic led to Lord Byron proposing that they all write a ghost story. Byron himself began a horrific tale about a vampire but quickly tired of it; Shelley, too, soon became bored with a strange, rambling story he attempted to weave about some of his childhood experiences; Polidori pegged away for a time at a novel about a skull-headed lady who spied on people through keyholes; and only Mary had to admit, morning after morning when she was chaffed on the subject, that she had failed even to make a beginning ... 'Then came an evening when Byron and Shelley were arguing about the nature and principle of life and wondering whether there was any possibility of this being discovered. They went on to discuss Dr Darwin's [grandfather of Charles Darwin] experiment in which he kept a piece of vermicelli in a glass case until for some unknown reason it began to wriggle to and fro. Neither poet felt that real life could be given in such a way, but they did think that life might be restored to a corpse by galvanic or similar methods, and that it might be possible to make and assemble the component parts of some creature and imbue the whole with the necessary vital warmth.'

In Mary Shelley's own words:

> Night waned upon this talk, and even the witching hour had gone by, before we retired to rest. When I placed my head on my pillow, I did not sleep, nor could I be said to think. My imagination, unbidden, possessed and guided me, gifting the successive images that arose in my mind with a vividness far beyond the usual bounds of reverie. I saw – with shut eyes, but acute mental vision – I saw the pale student of unhallowed arts kneeling

beside the thing he had put together, I saw the hideous phantasm of a man stretched out, and then, on the working of some powerful engine, show signs of life, and stir with an uneasy, half vital motion. Frightful must it be; for supremely frightful would be the effect of any human endeavour to mock the stupendous mechanism of the Creator of the world. His success would terrify the artist; he would rush away from his odious handiwork, horror-stricken. He would hope that, left to itself, the slight spark of life which he had communicated would fade; that this thing which had received such imperfect animation, would subside into dead matter; and he might sleep in the belief that the silence of the grave would quench forever the transient existence of the hideous corpse which he had looked upon as the cradle of life. He sleeps; but he is awakened; he opens his eyes; behold the horrid thing stands at his bedside, opening his curtains, and looking at him with yellow, watery, but speculative eyes. I opened mine in terror. The idea so possessed my mind that a thrill of fear ran through me, and I wished to exchange the ghastly image of my fancy for the realities around. I see them still; the very room, the dark *parquet*, the closed shutters, with the moonlight struggling through, and the sense I had that the glassy lake and the white high Alps were beyond. I could not so easily get rid of my hideous phantom; still it haunted me. I must try to think of something else. I recurred to my ghost story – my tiresome unlucky ghost story! On the morrow I announced that I had *thought of a story*. I began that day with the words, 'It was a dreary night of November,' making only a transcript of the grim terrors of my waking dream . . .

Mary planned to write a short story but when Shelley heard the theme he encouraged her to write a full-length novel; a book that was to give her immortality. So was *Frankenstein* born, the story with a touch of genius which has earned it a deserved and permanent place in English literature; it was indeed a remarkable achievement for a girl of nineteen.

There are several stories of how Karloff obtained the monster part and reading between the lines from various sources, including Karloff himself, I have arrived at what I think was the sequence of events. Mrs Karloff tells me she is not so sure. She first saw *Frankenstein* only a few years ago when some friends ran it through for her and Boris, who used to say in later years: 'My wife is a woman of great taste; she has seen very, very few of my pictures!'

When Universal first contemplated a film of *Frankenstein*, Robert Florey, the brilliant French director, had been assigned by the studio's story editor, Richard Schayer, to produce a storyline from the book, but Florey had made camera tests with Bela Lugosi, utilising the still-standing sets of *Dracula*, and the direction was entrusted to the British director James Whale, whose two films *Journey's End* (which he had also staged in London and New York) and *Waterloo Bridge* had shown great promise. Whale was a highly sophisticated man with a streak of strange humour which often came out in his work. He left the film industry in 1941 in puzzling circumstances, and was found drowned in his Hollywood swimming pool in 1957. He had noticed Karloff in *Graft*, and seeing the actor eating a meagre lunch in the commissary one day while casting *Frankenstein*, Whale called him over to his table for a cup of coffee. The outcome of their conversation was that Whale decided to give Karloff a test for the part of the monster.

Bela Lugosi would not countenance the onerous make-up that the role demanded and he disliked the part because the heavy make-up rendered him unrecognisable; however he did eventually play the Frankenstein monster in *Frankenstein Meets the Wolf Man* (1943). Karloff got the part and that, as he put it, 'kicked the goal for me.' 'The part was what we call a "natural," ' he used to add modestly, 'any actor who played it was destined for success.' Be that as it may, Karloff made *Frankenstein* the greatest 'horror' film of the talkies.

Karloff and a brilliant make-up man, Jack Pierce, worked together for three hours most evenings for three weeks creating the make-up for the monster, which eventually Universal copyrighted. With padding they built an enormous body around Karloff's own, an immense amount of nose-putty being applied to his features. A high, artificial skull was built up and eventually the creation gave an impression of tremendous strength. Finally, James Whale saw the test and was overjoyed. In 1957 Karloff said: 'Jack Pierce's words still echo in my mind: "This is going to be a big thing." How right he was.'

Willingly Karloff endured the hardships that came with this amazing role; the five hours it took to apply the grotesque make-up, the heavy disguise that endangered his health, the nut and bolt-like plugs embedded in his flesh . . . He struggled under the weight of some sixty pounds of accessories, including the double-domed skull (the bony ridges where the skull plates were joined being plainly visible); his shoes weighed eighteen pounds apiece – a lot of excess weight to carry around for something like eighteen hours at a stretch. Altogether, he wore so much extraneous material that an iron stand-in was used. This consisted of a girder mounted on a handtruck and wearing a mask resembling the monster! After each day's shooting, extensive massage and infra-red treatment was necessary to get Karloff's cramped and weary muscles back into shape.

Helen Weigel Brown described the enormous problems and difficulties in *Picturegoer*, date 23rd April 1932:

> When the directors told Jack Pierce that they were going to screen Boris Karloff in *Frankenstein*, and that they wanted something different in a super-horrifying monster, he hurried out and got the book, because he presumed, of course, that there would be a good description there from which he could begin to build his own idea of make-up for the part. But not at all. The author had neglected to describe the monster created by a young doctor out of the parts of dead bodies, except to say that he was of enormous size, and very, very horrible to look at.
>
> So the make-up man had to do a little researching on his own – and it took three and one-half months before he was satisfied with what he found.

He read all sorts of medical books – he talked with physicians and surgeons; sketching with them his ideas.

'What would a man look like whose brain had been taken from the head of another man, "transplanted" as it were? . . . What sort of a scar would an operation on the neck leave?' he demanded. 'How would a hand appear that had been "grafted" on to another arm? . . . How would this creature's hands appear if, when the electric spark of life was sent into the body, this life force failed to reach the ends of his fingers? . . . How would the eyes of a dead man appear if they were suddenly to open? . . .'

The colour of the skin was particularly difficult to get just right. Something that would screen like the pallor of a dead man – grey-white, which would have served the purpose on the stage, did not give the right effect under the Klieg lights. Neither did the yellowish tones. A dead, greenish-grey finally passed the test – the seventh one. The impression of 'dead' finger tips was given by the use of black make-up.

Each time the monster was created, Karloff had to sit in the make-up chair for three and a half hours. First his eyes had to be given that heavy, half-dead, insane look – a matter of applying coats and coats of wax to his eyelids to weigh them down. Next invisible wire clamps were fixed over his lips to pull the corners of his mouth out and down. Then the overhanging brow and high, square-shaped crown of the head, supposedly 'grafted' from the head of another man. These, as well as his

face and neck, were shaped and built up by means
of thin layers of cotton, applied with a special
liquid preparation so that it went on smoothly like
so many thin layers of flesh. Then the greyish
make-up on top of all. Bolt-like plugs were placed
on the side of the neck and held there by means of
more layers of cotton and adhesive liquids. For a
long time afterwards Karloff bore two small scars
on his neck, where the bolts had been fastened.

An assistant who helped apply the monster's
features stood by every moment the picture was
being filmed, for emergency repair work on the
make-up. Sometimes it was an eyelid that came
loose – another time the wig would slip in a fight,
or one of the heavy bolts would work loose in a
particularly frenzied scene.

Removing the make-up was not much simpler
than putting it on, and certainly more painful.
It required an hour and a half of prying, pulling
and coaxing, plus special oils and acids; 'plus a
great deal of bad language!' adds Karloff. First the
eyelids came off – most painful, to say the least;
and enough to inspire any quantity of questionable
language! The deep scar on the monster's forehead
was then pried into as a good starting point, and
from then it was just one pry and push and acid
soaking after another until Boris was himself
again . . .

Jack Pierce himself described how he created the
monster make-up in a *New York Times* interview in 1939.

. . . I didn't depend on imagination. Before I did
any designing I did some research in anatomy,

surgery, criminology, ancient and modern burial customs, and electrodynamics. I discovered that there are six ways a surgeon can cut the skull and I figured Dr Frankenstein, who was not a practising surgeon, would take the easiest. That is, he would cut the top of the skull off straight across like a pot lid, hinge it, pop the brain in, and clamp it tight. That's the reason I decided to make the monster's head square and flat like a box and dig that big scar across his forehead and have metal clamps hold it together. The two metal studs that stuck out of the sides of his neck were inlets for electricity – plugs; not bolts. Don't forget the monster was an electrical gadget and that lightning was his life force . . . Also I had read that the Egyptians used to bind some criminals hand and foot and bury them alive. When their blood turned to water after their death, it flowed into their extremities and stretched their arms to gorilla length and swelled their hands and feet and faces to abnormal proportions. I thought this would make a nice touch for the monster, since he was supposed to be made from the corpses of executed felons. So I fixed Karloff up that way. The lizard eyes were made of rubber, as was his false head. I made his arms look longer by shortening the sleeves of his coat. His legs were stiffened by steel struts and two pairs of trousers. His large feet were the boots asphalt-spreaders wear. His finger-nails were blackened with shoe polish . . .

Jack Pierce himself was quite a character: in 1910 he was a promising 'shortstop' in baseball and he went

to California, from Chicago, to break into the Coast
League baseball team, not into the movies! But he was
too light for the team and he took a cinema projectionist
job, later managing theatres for Harry Culver, the
founder of Culver City. Then, with Young Deer, the
Indian producer, he began making pictures, and in 1914
joined Universal as assistant cameraman. He moved
to make-up and one of his first grotesque transformations
was to make a monkey out of Jacques Lerner in *The
Monkey Talks* for Fox Pictures! In 1926 he went back
to Universal and for the rest of his life used his small,
muscular fingers to make human faces more beautiful,
or more horrible, than nature intended.

Karloff's make-up for *Frankenstein* was guarded care-
fully; so much so that he made the journeys between
his dressing-room and the set wrapped in sheets. The
producer wanted it to be a surprise and a shudder even
to Hollywood. There is a story that on the day shooting
was due to begin, Universal's Frank Whitbeck took his
chief, Carl Laemmle, round the sets where *Frankenstein*
was to be filmed, and as the odd pair walked away
afterwards, the giant Whitbeck noticed that the tiny
Laemmle was unusually quiet. Suddenly they came to a
halt and Laemmle turned to Whitbeck. 'I'm issuing
orders,' he said, 'that Mr Karloff must always have his
face covered when he walks around the lot.' 'But why,
Mr Laemmle?' asked Whitbeck, puzzled. 'Because,'
replied Laemmle, with soft emphasis, 'some of our nice
little secretaries are pregnant and they might be
frightened if they saw him!'

Throughout the long hours of shooting the scenes and
all through the rest periods, Karloff had to keep his

make-up on, though he did have the opportunity now and again between scenes to doff his padded suit and massive feet, and if he was very careful he could enjoy the luxury of a hastily-puffed cigarette. The film was shot during hot weather and was a gruelling task for Karloff. The sheer physical activity was so great that at times he acted in a sopping-wet undersuit.

In *Frankenstein* the monster could not speak; he was an artificial living creature, made from bits and pieces of human bodies by the scientist Frankenstein. Karloff regarded the role as a challenge and he portrayed in masterly fashion the sub-human creature of little intelligence, able only to utter a few guttural and animal noises; 'he talked with his eyes'. Yet he still got across the sympathetic qualities in the role. The monster appeared to be trying to grow a soul. His eyes begged for understanding. Relatively well-behaved at first, he was goaded by cruelty and without knowledge of right and wrong to become a killer and so he had to be destroyed. The twist whereby a madman's brain was used for the creation of the monster in place of the brain of a normal man was the idea of Robert Florey, then directing Bela Lugosi in *The Murders in the Rue Morgue*. No one, it has been said, who saw the film *Frankenstein* has ever been able to forget the monster's half-closed eyes; liquid, pleading, half-intelligent, peering through the outlandish make-up . . . Carl Laemmle once said: 'Karloff's eyes mirrored the suffering we needed'.

Because of the controversial theme of Baron Frankenstein playing at God the release date of the film was delayed, but it finally opened on 6th December 1931. At the first preview in the quiet community of Santa

Barbara, California, to which Karloff was not invited, many of the elegant ladies and well-groomed gentlemen got up and walked out at their first sight of Karloff as the monster. Much publicity was given to the fact that ambulances were in attendance to treat those who could not stand the shock. Many of those who left paced the sidewalk for a time, then went back into the theatre. They couldn't stand the picture and yet they couldn't leave it. James Whale recalls that the telephone rang at 2 am that night in his room at Santa Barbara's Biltmore Hotel, and an angry male voice said, 'I can't sleep on account of your picture, so I'm darned if you're going to sleep either. That's why I called you up!' The film cost Universal $275,000 to produce and brought the studio $12,000,000 in theatre rental. Percentagewise it was the most profitable movie ever made. When, in 1938, Universal reissued *Frankenstein* and *Dracula* together, the films brought in higher gross takings than in their original runs.

Another telephone was ringing at this time concerning the film everyone was talking about. Shortly after the film was released, Karloff's agent called him one morning and told him that a contract was being signed with Universal studios. Karloff heaved a sigh of relief: he had made it at last. An actor under contract, something he had always dreamed of in the dark days of extra work and bit parts.

The success of *Frankenstein* brought almost as much relief to Karloff's brothers. He remembered Ted writing, 'I hope you are saving every farthing you can lay your hands on, my boy, because obviously this can't go on much longer.' It went on much, much longer than anyone, including Karloff himself, thought possible.

In the film, the monster came on backwards for his first scene. When, finally, he turned around and let his face be seen, knees knocked together all over the cinema and a kind of collective groan went up. The impact was overwhelming. The monster's hand gestures were copied from Lon Chaney's in *The Trap* (1922). *Frankenstein* gave Karloff his big break, although many people would not have considered it a break for it established him as the possessor of the most frightening face in the world! Universal released a few prints of the film in green, 'the colour of fear' and the resulting, eerie quality encouraged other studios to experiment with colour in subsequent horror pictures.

One of the odd effects of Karloff's brilliant playing of the role was that while children everywhere loved the film and felt an instinctive sympathy for the monster, their parents, though fascinated, hated the picture. Karloff received hundreds of letters from children expressing pity for the poor creature. 'The children have never fallen for my nonsense,' said Karloff. 'They sit in the cinema with their eyes glued on the screen. They watch the monster parading his stuff, and now and then give hoots of mock terror or shiver with suppressed excitement, but the moment the word *END* flashes on the screen, they begin to laugh and chatter away about Karloff and his antics.'

'By the time they reach home they are ready to write me letters like this one,' Karloff told W H Mooring in 1937. The letter, one of many, came from a little girl. She said something like this: 'I always like to see you as

the Frankenstein monster, though at home they sometimes tell me it will make me sleep badly at nights.
It doesn't. If I lie awake thinking about you I think
what a poor, frightened thing you are with all those
people chasing you: besides, you didn't mean to be bad,
did you? They made you be.' The episode where a
little girl befriends the monster who murders her proved
to be too strong for the audiences of the day to accept
and the actual murder scene was deleted – the only
scene to be cut from the finished film which in its later
form shows the child and the monster together playing
with flowers by a lake and then, a little later, the child's
father is seen carrying the drowned body in his arms.

Karloff himself always had a respect for the monster
and did not like to have him made a butt of jokes; he
frequently refused to attend 'monster parties' at which
the monster was to be burlesqued. At the time of the
wartime box-office slump in horror pictures the promo-
tion men in America issued a dare to the public to sit
alone in a darkened movie theatre after midnight on
Hallowe'en through an entire screening of the original
Frankenstein. The prize was a $25 War Bond but I have
yet to hear of anyone who collected! This classic film,
which wears remarkably well, is shown to members of
the National Film Theatre in London from time to time
and it turned up on Independent Television in Britain
on 28th July 1969, taking me back thirty years to when
I first saw it double-billed with *Dracula* in 1939.

It was after Karloff had settled in England in 1959
that America saw on television a travesty of the Frankenstein monster when the creepy Charles Addams cartoons
came to life as *The Addams Family* (ABC) and later in a

television comedy film series entitled *The Munsters*, which featured a friendly family of well-known weirdies including the hero in Frankenstein monster make-up. The series first appeared on BBC television in 1965. It was a step that even the psychiatrists deplored. 'We are moving from the beautiful to the ugly' said one, prophetically.

In 1968 I asked Philip Jenkinson of BBC television's *Film Review* how he regarded Boris Karloff. 'As far as I am concerned Boris Karloff was the mainspring of the horror tradition,' he replied, 'bringing sensitivity and style to a *genre* that would surely have crumbled left to the lesser talents that jumped on the bandwagon. If Freund and Browning were the masterbuilders, then he was surely the architect. Without him – as was later evident – *Frankenstein* would have been nothing.'

All things considered it was perhaps understandable that Karloff had a real fondness for the *Frankenstein* monster and one of his most treasured possessions was an early edition of Mary Shelley's masterpiece. He was amused when I pointed out to him the Everyman's Library edition where Dr R E Dowse and D J Palmer's introduction begins, following a quotation from Mary Shelley: 'And so Boris Karloff looms out of the mists of our boyhood imaginations . . .'

Frankenstein is the most famous horror movie of all time; it was a story that enables Karloff to rise from the mediocrity of a film actor to the dizzy and demanding heights of a world-famous filmstar.

CHAPTER 6

Aftermath of Frankenstein

LOGICALLY SPEAKING, THE whole of the film career of Boris Karloff was the aftermath of *Frankenstein*; but it is pertinent to consider at this stage the immediate effect the film had on the cinema public of the day, and on that elusive but all-important facet of film-making: box-office demand.

No one appreciated more than Boris Karloff the importance of catering for what the public wants. Writing in *Films and Filming* in November 1957, he pointed out that 'this *genre* of film entertainment obviously fulfills a desire in people to experience something which is beyond the range of everyday human emotion . . . for millions of filmgoers they relieve the humdrum life of the average individual better than any other kind of story, and that after all is what entertainment should always do.'

When *Frankenstein* was first shown, as we have seen, people were fascinated; people were scared; but above all people were thrilled as they had never been thrilled by a film before. And they liked it. They wanted more. The film studios, and particularly Universal, saw that they got more. In her remarkable account of Hollywood in its heyday, *This was Hollywood* (1960), Beth Day reveals that Universal, Hollywood's first walled city, conceived and created by the imaginative but irresponsible Carl Laemmle, is now owned by the powerful MCA agency. One of the many photographs in Beth Day's volume shows Boris Karloff at one of his rare parties, partaking of the sixty-fifth birthday cake of little German-born Carl Laemmle.

So Karloff was at last kept busy. He created his success in a 'horror' film and had to continue his menacing in picture after picture. When *Frankenstein* was made, a horror film was something new; today horror pictures support a handful of independent producers who make only films of this kind. They don't even trouble with the conventional press-previews because these films have guaranteed, but limited, attendances and they rarely lose money, regardless of the opinions of film critics. It may well be that a lot of people owe a great deal to Karloff!

Frankenstein set the fashion for horror films. There had never been anything like it, with the questionable exception of Dr R Wiene's brilliant *The Cabinet of Dr Caligari*. Filmed at the height of the expressionist movement, this story told of the fantastically-imagined murder in an asylum for the insane by a patient: an attempt to portray the world and its inhabitants as seen through the eyes of a madman. It was a German master-piece with settings and camera-work far in advance of its time. The film was picked by one hundred and seventeen film historians from twenty-six countries as one of the first twelve best films of all time, for presentation during the last week of the Brussels Exhibition in 1958.

73

Caligari, with its masterly direction, was the forerunner of all horror films. If one could say that the horror film arrived in two steps, the first step was *Caligari* in 1919 and the second *Frankenstein* in 1931. *Frankenstein*, and in no small degree, Karloff's brilliant portrayal of the ambling and forlorn monster, was undoubtedly the start of the wave of horror pictures in the 'thirties. Although somewhat uneven, the film is almost noble in its special effects and in its respect for the unknown.

The word horror, incidentally, is a misnomer, as Karloff himself repeatedly pointed out, for it means revulsion. The films he made were made for entertainment, maybe with the object of making the audiences' hair stand on end, but never to revolt people. He always preferred the word terror, which, he used to say, indicates good, clean, scary fun . . . but alas, it is too late now to change the adjective. His films prompted the British Censor to introduce a certificate in the early 'thirties known as 'H' – for horror, a category that was withdrawn in 1956. So although he disliked the word horror, it is a word that was tagged to him for life.

In his article in the November 1957 issue of *Films and Filming*, Karloff suggested that the fascination of the horror film is because of the unknown and what might be. 'Most people like to pretend that there is something just behind the door,' he said, 'it transports the audience to another world. A world of fantasy and imagination. A world inhabited by the characters of Hans Andersen and the Brothers Grimm. The horror film is concocted more or less from the folk tales of every country and when I am asked if these films are harmful to children, my answer is always the same: do Grimms' fairy tales

74

do any harm to children? I never heard of fairy tale books being used in evidence in a juvenile delinquency court!' Psychologists recognise the value of horror films and Dr Zelda Wolpe of the University of Southern California is quoted as saying 'horror films build up, then release, tension, and this may help children to overcome real life anxiety.'

On this point I was amused to read the views that appeared in the 'Behind the Lines' column in *The Bookseller*, 21st March 1959. Headed 'Father to Man' the contributor stated: 'I have been pondering for some time some remarks made by Mr Herman Cohen, a recent visitor to these shores from Hollywood. There is, I feel sure, a moral in them somewhere. Mr Cohen, who is a film producer, was upset by the British 'X' certificate given to films thought to be unsuitable for children. "It is wrong," he told the *Evening Standard*, "children of all ages should be allowed to see horror films. I am sure that *Frankenstein* and *Dracula* would not have any serious effect on children's minds. After all, I saw them myself when I was a kid and they didn't affect me." Mr Cohen, I learn, was responsible for the film called *I Was a Teenage Werewolf*. His latest works are *Horrors of the Black Museum* and *The Headless Ghost*. Perhaps he didn't notice the effect!'

The Karloff film released immediately after *Frankenstein* was *Tonight or Never*, with Gloria Swanson and Melvyn Douglas. Karloff, as a waiter, had a very funny scene in this film but it was too soon after *Frankenstein* for him to register as the same actor. About this time, *Business and Pleasure* was released with the much-loved Will Rogers; a 'spoof' on the currently popular desert pictures with Karloff as a sheik and Will Rogers a visiting razorblade king from Oklahoma. *Alias the Doctor* appeared the following year with its prophetic casting of Karloff as an autopsy surgeon who was disappointed whenever an operation was successful!

Then, released in 1933, came *Scarface*, directed by Howard Hawks for United Artists; a gangster film starring Paul Muni and George Raft in a story of wholesale shootings and bitter, relentless warfare waged between rival American gangs in Prohibition days. It is still generally regarded as the best of all gangster films; brutal, ruthless and painfully realistic with admirable direction and brilliant acting from the supporting cast which, in addition to Boris Karloff, included Karen Morley and Ann Dvorak. This film, from the novel by Armitage Trail, was re-issued in 1938. Gaylord Lloyd, one of the directors of the film, lost an eye during the shooting of the gangster massacre in the garage. The method of touching off dynamite caps was used for the machine-gun fire and this method was always dangerous owing to the copper in the caps scattering and the inevitable flying splinters. Paul Muni played Tony Camonte (modelled after Al Capone), and Karloff was Gaffney, a rival mobster who was shot down while bowling. The ball knocks down all the pins but one, then that one finally topples over.

Karloff had an unusual opportunity in another film he made around this time, *Cohens and the Kellys in Hollywood*, for in this Universal film, directed by John Francis Dillon, the two families meet Karloff, playing himself, in a restaurant. Karloff was delighted to appear next in *The Miracle Man* (1932) although he was back in one of his more usual roles. The film was directed by Norman Z McLeod, and starred John Wray, Chester Morris and Sylvia Sydney. It was in fact a remake of the classic silent-film that told the story of three men and a girl who decide to exploit a faith-healer, originally directed by George Tucker for Paramount in 1919, a film that made stars of its three principals: Lon Chaney, Betty Compson and Thomas Meighan. In the 1932 version, John Wray had the Lon Chaney part and Karloff appeared as Nikko, the shrewd charlatan who ran a fake healing mission.

Karloff was next seen in the Jack Holt, Constance Cummings film, *Behind the Mask*, a mystery story of the secret service and the breaking-up of a narcotics ring; then in *The Mummy* (Universal, 1932) with Zita Johann and David Manners and directed by Karl Freund, the brilliant cameraman of *Dracula* and *Murders in the Rue Morgue*. Freund went on to direct Peter Lorre in that distinguished actor's American debut in *The Hands of Orlac* (also entitled *Mad Love*), after which Freund resumed his camera work with outstanding success and never directed another film.

Karloff once said that he had probably used more beauty clay than any half-dozen women in the United States of America; and indeed he literally wallowed in tons of it! For *The Mummy*, a coating of it was put all over his body. Blue-green in colour because it photographed a graveyard grey. When dry it was like wearing a plaster cast; he could scarcely move a muscle and even talking became a tremendous effort. On the surface, the mud broke into thousands of hair-line cracks that looked like wrinkles. Make-up artists went over every one of these cracks with thin brushes and accented them with paint; then 'veins' were pasted on the surface by soaking strips of cotton in collodion! The make-up for Karloff's part of the ancient mummy, Imhotep, in the early part of the film took eight hours to assume; in the later scenes he played an Egyptian priest. One of the most celebrated scenes of all horror films has Karloff, as the mummy coming back to life after 3,700 years and finding in a young English girl the reincarnation of the Egyptian princess he had loved in antiquity. Although this film did much to confirm for some people Karloff as Chaney's successor in horror roles, the much publicised mummy make-up was seen on the screen only briefly, and most of the time Karloff played the parchment-faced archaeologist: enigmatic and stiff; one of his more restrained performances. Excellent editing by Milton Carruth, magnificent lighting by Charles Stumar (obviously influenced by Freund), and a superb performance by Karloff made this a horror classic almost without equal.

Also in 1932 came *Night World*, in which several stories were concocted into a tale about a nightclub owner, played by Karloff in a sympathetic role. *The Mask of Fu Manchu* (MGM, 1932) followed, with Lewis Stone and Karen Morley. Directed by Charles Brabin and Charles Vidor the film was based on the sinister and inscrutable, oriental villain Dr Fu Manchu, created by Sax Rohmer and combined a number of incidents from that author's string of exotic thrillers. I asked Sax Rohmer for his opinion of this film and Karloff's characterisation. He told me that unfortunately he was in Egypt when the film was exhibited and he never saw it but he added: 'Boris Karloff would be an ideal choice for Fu Manchu.' A S Ward (Sax Rohmer) once told me that the character of Fu Manchu was based on a real-life Limehouse gangster and he suspected that the long list of Egyptian mummy-films was probably inspired by the discovery of Tutankhamen's tomb in 1922 and by the reputed curse that fell on all those who unearthed the mummy and desecrated the fabulous wealth of the tomb. After Sax Rohmer died in 1959 his widow presented me with an Egyptian ushanti figure from the collection which he so loved, as a memento of her husband; he had bought it in Egypt on their honeymoon in 1913. Boris Karloff would have enjoyed knowing Sax Rohmer whose remarkable knowledge of the East and its mysteries was unrivalled.

The same year saw Karloff in *The Old Dark House* (Universal) from J B Priestley's novel *The Benighted*; this film was directed by James (*Frankenstein*) Whale who by now had become accepted as Universal's 'master of horror' and this film explored fully the wit, elegance and sharp characterisation of which Whale was superbly capable. For his part as the mute butler, in the strange house filled with madmen, Karloff wore a beard and a scar over the right eye from eyebrow to hairline. Acting with such renowned and established players as Charles Laughton, Raymond Massey, Melvyn Douglas and Ernest Thesiger, Karloff stood out with his disturbing portrayal in this thriller which was reissued in 1945. As Pierre Artis puts it in his *Histoire du Cinéma Américain* (1947), Karloff 'who remains one of the most peaceful actors in Hollywood, terrified, with all his talents, visitors to *The Old Dark House*.'

As Carlos Clarens relates in *Horror Movies* (1968), *The Old Dark House* concerns the Femms who emerge as a parody of the traditional English family; a bedridden century-old patriarch (listed in the cast as John Dudgeon but actually played by an old crone); his sexagenarian son (Ernest Thesiger), obsessed with maintaining decorum at all costs; his fanatically religious sister (Eva Moore) who frequently calls upon her God; and a younger brother (Brember Wills) a pyromaniac dwarf who is kept behind locked doors. Karloff, as Morgan, a scarred brute of a man – half butler, half keeper – is not to be trusted near a bottle of liquor or an attractive female. During the night, when a group of travellers are forced to seek shelter, the old, dark house reveals its secrets.

Karloff turned down Whale's follow-up, the successful adaptation of H G Wells' story *The Invisible Man* (1933) and the part was taken by Claud Rains. Instead, Karloff came to Britain to appear in *The Ghoul* (Gaumont-British), regarded by many film students as one of Karloff's best films. Directed by T Hayes Hunter and with a strong cast including Sir Cedric Hardwicke and Dorothy Hyson, Karloff played a dual-role of the half-mad recluse, Professor Edward Morlant, and a master criminal known as 'the Ghoul', an expert at disguise who impersonates the Professor after murdering him. This exciting and fast-moving film had *all* the ingredients one could wish for in a creepy, thrilling, murder-mystery: strange footsteps and attempted murder in the swirling fog of London; a huge, sombre house in Yorkshire miles from anywhere; secret tunnels; screams in the night; a tremendous conflagration at the end with the hero and heroine seemingly imprisoned without hope of escape in a concealed priesthole; brutal murder and an indescribable air of suspense. Karloff himself gave a masterly performance and was ably supported by a fine cast. The result was a truly memorable film. I have a copy of the book of the film – now something of a collector's item.

In the years that followed *Frankenstein*, Karloff was to appear in many (some people thought too many) films of a similar character and while some of the films were no more than mediocre, others were very good indeed. Among the films in the latter category that gave the discerning filmgoer the opportunity of seeing Karloff act as well as shock, *The Ghoul* is generally regarded as outstanding by film-critics and the filmgoing public alike. It was fitting that his first trip to Britain in twenty-four years resulted in such a successful film. On his arrival in England on this occasion three of his distinguished brothers: Sir John Pratt, former Vice-Consul in China, Consul in the Far East and in charge of all Chinese affairs at the Foreign Office (retired 1938); Mr Justice E M Pratt, retired, formerly Judge of the High Court of Bombay and Mr F G Pratt, csi, retired, formerly of the Executive Branch of the Indian Civil Service, a member of the Viceroy's staff and for a long time Governor of a province in India, were among the many guests at a reception given for Karloff who liked to tell an amusing little story about this trip.

It seems that a leading newspaper had sent a photographer to secure pictures of some of the notables present and finally the cameraman asked the actor to pose with his brothers. 'This was the moment I had been dreading,'

Karloff said. 'I felt that they would consider it beneath their dignity and expected to be told in no uncertain terms that such a thing was impossible. But I hunted them up and put the proposition to them. "I realise," I said apologetically, "that I make my living in a rather queer fashion, and I only bring this to your notice because the man is so insistent. I assure you that it is not an idea of my own, but – well, there is a photographer here who wants to take our picture together".'

' "Where is he?" asked Sir John, excitedly. "Bring him in here and let's be photographed in front of this fireplace!" They were as pleased as three boys, and when the photographer had come in from the other room they began to argue as to where each should stand. Finally it was decided that we should all line up according to age, with my brother John at one end and myself on the other. No sooner was the picture taken than all three brothers began to enquire how soon they could secure prints – and by this time I was in a positive glow of relief. A film actor had been received in British diplomatic circles and had made good!'

'I must tell you,' he said to me in London in 1968, as he had once told Maurice Ruddy, 'of the loveliest thing that occurred during this visit. It was late on Friday that we arrived at Southampton. I was terribly excited, of course, to be back home after twenty-four years. It was really thrilling to be on English soil once more. I wanted to see London and to know all about the changes. I drove all over London with my brothers, and it gave me one of the greatest moments of my life . . .

'Then, with the Gleasons, I went to Drury Lane. My wife, who had never been to England before, had arranged for a quiet evening, and she told no one that we were going to the theatre. Yet somehow people got to know. A tremendous crowd had gathered round the entrance. As I got out of the cab, many of them shouted in a most friendly fashion: "Welcome home, Mr Karloff, welcome home." They came around, some wanting autographs, some more simply to extend friendly greetings . . .

'A welcome to me! I was overcome almost to the point of tears. Then a man in the crowd came to the rescue. "It's all right, Mr Karloff, we'll wait until after the show. This is a good play. We don't want you to miss any of it. You go into the theatre with your party and we'll be waiting after the performance." It was terribly touching to have extended to me those lovely sentiments and that great kindness and consideration, which came from the heart . . .

'They were waiting for me after the show. I was deeply impressed with their friendly good will, and I realised what a great thing, literally beyond price, is the friendship of the people. Somehow, I feel it could have happened only in London and was fully representative of the heart of its people, of my people . . .

'The meeting again with my brothers was quite different from what I had anticipated. There was a little difference in my suddenly having attained fame, when my mature family had taken years to establish themselves in their respective diplomatic posts; but Jack immediately put me at my ease by saying: "It's simply grand and we're all delighted to see you come home in triumph." . . .

'I have often thought how absurd and lopsided it is

that men like my brothers should spend their lives in
the service of their country, and be comparatively
unknown, whereas I, because of a series of lucky accidents, have been granted fame and some fortune. Anything I have achieved in my life in no way compares to
anything they or the hundreds of men like them have
done . . .

'The twenty-odd years we had been apart made a
difference. The strangeness had to wear off. We had to
find the common touch. Then there came that lovely
sense of well-being, of deep understanding and warm
friendship.' . . . And yet it wasn't all as it might have
been. Soon after returning to Hollywood ('my work is
here, my struggles have been here – and all the friend-
ships that belong to my maturity'), he gave an interview
in which he related how, for the first few days, he and his
brothers had chattered like magpies but then conversation and recollections began to run low and when they
tried to continue, they were struck by the fact that they
had nothing more to say to each other; they had no
common ground of experience. 'Absence makes strangers
of the closest relatives,' he mused.

I asked him why, if he was so fond of England, he had
not been back before. His answer, like so much about
this intelligent but uncomplicated man, was simple:
'When I was working, I couldn't find the time. When I
wasn't working, I couldn't find the money.' It seemed to
me that those two sentences covered a great deal of
home-sickness, and Karloff was understandably disappointed that he had to rush back to Hollywood to
fulfil a contract.

The year 1934 saw Karloff in *The House of Doom*
(entitled *The Black Cat* in America) with Bela Lugosi

and directed by Edgar G Ulmer for Universal; a well-acted, well-photographed and thrilling film which had nothing to do with Edgar Allan Poe's sinister short-story *The Black Cat*. In this first film in which Karloff appeared with Lugosi, sharing equal billing and screen time, Karloff played the head of a devil-worshipping cult who lived in a modernistic castle built over the ruins of a still-mined battlefield. Lugosi returns after fifteen years as a prisoner of war to find his daughter has become Karloff's mistress, while his wife's body has been preserved as a trophy in the vaults, giving rise to the alleged necrophilian element in the film. The climax consisted of Karloff about to officiate at a Black Mass with the participation of an unwilling victim, when Lugosi steps in and Karloff finds himself tied to a rack and skinned alive just before the whole castle blows up!

In contrast, his next film, *Gift of Gab*, also for Universal, gave Karloff a small 'natural' part in a film where the plot served as an excuse for introducing American radio-stars. The film was really a series of turns with a crime-play background. The players included Edmund Lowe.

Then came *The Lost Patrol* (RKO) directed by John Ford, a highly regarded and unusual film which many people found strangely moving, with Karloff giving a vivid and memorable portrayal as a religious fanatic, a member of a British army patrol lost among the sandhills of Mesopotamia. *The Lost Patrol* was reissued in 1949. It creaked badly when shown on British television a few years ago. This film was made in the Yuma desert under a sun that generated heat of 150 degrees in the shade, and work was limited to two hours a day;

even so half the company (all men) were prostrate at one time or another. Karloff's big moment in the film came towards the end where a sharp-shooter outlined his feet with bullets at a range of twenty yards – as he walked along! Karloff was supposed to have been driven insane by the heat and by the time the location team packed up for home, he very nearly was!

The actors with whom he was appearing at this time may be taken as an indication of Karloff's acting ability. In *The Lost Patrol* he shared honours with Victor McLaglen and Reginald Denny, and in the film that followed Karloff appeared with the great George Arliss, then at the height of his fame, Robert Young, Loretta Young and Karloff's friend C Aubrey Smith. The film, *The House of Rothschild*, was produced by 20th-Century, distributed by United Artists, and directed by Alfred Werker. This excursion into costume for Karloff gave filmgoers the opportunity of seeing him in sideburns and high collar for this story of the fortunes of the powerful banking family of Rothschild during the Napoleonic Wars. Towards the end of the film there was a sequence in Technicolor – a reception by the Prince Regent – and altogether *The House of Rothschild* was considered to be one of the outstanding films of the year. Karloff's contribution was notable and added another fine performance to his fast-growing list of varied roles. It also widened his audience; those who had not noticed him previously, simply because they did not find 'horror' films to their liking, suddenly 'discovered' a new face and a new actor.

But before we look further at the many film parts that kept Karloff in the front rank of character actors, let us turn for a moment and look at his personal life.

CHAPTER 7

The Hobbies and Private Life
of a 'Monster'

To MANY PEOPLE it appeared that by 1936 Boris Karloff, the man they called 'the gentle monster', had begun to look upon America as his home. He was now married to Dorothy Stine, a librarian in the Los Angeles public school system and a graduate of the University of Southern California. They lived high up in the lovely country estate of Cold Water Canyon and had created what has been described as 'a little piece of England', where prize Bedlington terriers raced back and forth over the terraced lawns and the Karloffs indulged their love of gardening and pets.

Karloff, himself, worked out the plan for the flower beds and for the plots of lawn and the vine-covered slopes in the estate of several acres, and when not working at the studios he would frequently be found, wearing a faded pair of dungarees and an old shirt, digging, mowing and weeding and indeed working generally on what he liked to call 'the little farm.'

W H Mooring, the well-known film writer, visited the Karloffs at this time and writing in *Film Weekly* in 1937 he described his approach to the Karloff domain as he left below him Hollywood and beautiful Beverly Hills, turned into a shady canyon and climbed up a winding hillside bordered with eucalyptus and honeysuckle. The long, sloping hillside turned out to be just part of the actor's huge garden, and there striding towards him with the mechanical, familiar gait was the tall, gaunt figure of Boris Karloff himself, his sympathetic, brown eyes, his disarming smile, the soft, well-trained voice bidding his visitor welcome to a rambling Mexican-style farmhouse. The Karloff household, filled with interesting pieces (many bought during visits to England), was almost hidden from the road. Here with the three frisky terriers; two frolicsome Scotties ('Whisky' and 'Soda'!); a four-hundred pound pig named Violet; a pair of ducks; a number of chickens; an aged turtle and a parrot, its chain clanking as it banged against pewter beermugs in the typically English bar, Mooring found Karloff to be a friendly, cheerful and kindly man who bore no resemblance to the roles he customarily enacted. Many of the animals had been presented by fellow actors and actresses who knew how much Karloff loved all living things. He was especially fond of children and they, like critics, instinctively responded to him, sensing the intelligent, sincere quality behind the quiet smile and the gentle voice.

Previously, the Karloffs had lived on the shore of Toluca Lake, and Boris and his wife enjoyed feeding the wild ducks, walking their dogs in the brief, Californian twilight and dining upon such English dishes as roast beef and Yorkshire-pudding – to the sound of Noel Coward records. On Sundays, Karloff would indulge his endless passion for cricket and play at the Hollywood

Cricket Club where members included such actors as C Aubrey Smith, Clive Brook, Conway Tearle and Ronald Colman. While living there he had a dusty Ford with *Hollywood Cricket Club* emblazoned proudly on the tyre cover!

From a host of examples here are just a few incidents which reflect Karloff's character and love of children. Once, in Hollywood, a group of children, who must have realised that it was not unknown for him to drop whatever he was doing to play with children, rang his doorbell one Hallowe'en and asked him to go out with them and frighten their neighbours! Reluctantly, but with his customary charm, he turned down this offer of using his talents! In the minds of these children he could hardly have been the bogyman he so often portrayed in films. On more than one occasion Karloff travelled many miles to play Father Christmas at parties for crippled children and at hospitals. On television and film sets small children have approached him timidly and begged to be photographed with him. After the picture was shot, Karloff would ask solicitously: 'Are you still in one piece?' and the children would squirm with delight!

In his article in *Films and Filming* in 1957, Karloff said: 'Perhaps the best possible audience for a "horror" film is a child audience. The vivid imagination with which a child is gifted is far more receptive to the ingredients in these pictures than the adult imagination which merely finds them artificial. Because they have vivid imaginations we must not underestimate children . . . they know far more than we think they do. When I played Frankenstein's monster I received sack loads of fan mail . . . mostly from young girls. These children had seen right through the make-up and had been deeply moved by sympathy for the poor brute.'

The deep-set eyes that looked out from so many weird make-ups were in fact those of one of the mildest of men. So considerate was he of other peoples' feelings that for years secretaries in the offices of the American Screen Actors Guild used to refer to him as 'Dear Boris' as if that were his name; they would even leave messages, saying, for example: 'Dear Boris called today.'

Boris Karloff was always extremely modest and perhaps a little shy, but agile-minded, quick-witted and beautifully eloquent. He felt that his life away from the theatre and film studio should be his private territory. He was never interested in telling the world about himself and in fact he appeared to be slightly sceptical that anyone should want to know about him. I have lost count of the number of times I tried to arouse his interest in this biography. Later he told me that when he lived in Hollywood (and he lived there as a lorry-driver; as an extra; a bit player and as a star) he lived entirely his own life. He didn't go to nightclubs or parties because they didn't interest him and he rarely attended movie parties or premières, although, as he put it: 'When I do, no great calamity strikes the hand that shakes mine(!)'. But he was sometimes seen at consular receptions, at cricket, soccer or rugby matches, or at occasional gatherings of the so-called British colony.

It is perhaps significant that although he lived in Hollywood, at that time and for years both before and after, the very hub of the cinema industry of the world, Boris Karloff was yet essentially an Englishman. In an article on Hollywood's Foreign Colony by Frank Daughterty, published in the Boston *Christian Science*

Monitor, 3rd June 1936, Karloff is referred to as one of the 'prominent English people who now make their homes in Hollywood.' 'British customs notoriously prevail among the British colony,' we are told. 'Speaking a language which at least approximates that of the Americans, they maintain a stricter aloofness than do most other nationalities, are harder to absorb, even after years. Several English cake shops exist and cater almost exclusively to English trade. Once a year, on New Year's Eve, the principal members of the British colony gather at a Hollywood cafe to hear the bells of Big Ben ring out over the radio. . .' Karloff told me that he did not know much about this 'British Colony', although he had heard the phrase. He obviously didn't believe it really existed, although of course there were a lot of English actors, like Ronald Colman whom he knew slightly, Clive Brook, who tells me he never actually met Karloff and the late C Aubrey Smith whom he knew extremely well – simply because they had tastes in common. He played a lot of cricket with Aubrey Smith and kept in touch with Mrs Smith until she died, aged over 90, in 1969; always visiting her whenever he and his wife went to California. In the dining room-cum-study of the Karloff flat in London there hang two fine early paintings on glass of cricketing subjects that once belonged to Aubrey Smith.

Cricket was always Karloff's great sporting interest. Aubrey Smith, who was much older than Karloff, had introduced the game to Hollywood, and they both played for the Hollywood Cricket Club and became great friends. Sir C Aubrey Smith was the undisputed king of Hollywood's cricket-loving English colony and he and Karloff once represented the film capital against a touring Australian team that included Bradman and McCabe. 'They hid me in the slips', Karloff told me, modestly. He always followed avidly the fortunes of British cricket, frequently travelling many miles to attend test matches where his tall figure and characteristic walk was a familiar sight; and he was seen, too, at small local matches. He once umpired a charity match at Hitchin in Hertfordshire. The proceeds from the match were highly satisfactory and since John Arlott has reminded us that an umpire is the only single person who can, alas, make or mar a cricket match, there is little doubt that Karloff's handling of that game as well as his presence was responsible for the success. On more than one occasion when being interviewed in England, he cut short the interrogation in the nicest possible way, explaining that he had to be off 'to see Surrey at the Oval.'

There is or was another Karloff in American show business, a man who signed himself, 'Boris Karloff Jnr' but Boris Karloff had no son and 'Tony Karloff' was no relation whatever. Many years ago a young man had written to Boris Karloff to ask whether he could use the name in connection with a mystery stage act and since Karloff attributed no particular importance to the name, he readily gave the necessary permission.

A daughter, Sara Jane, was born to Boris Karloff and Dorothy Stine on Karloff's fifty-first birthday, in 1938, when he was working on *Son of Frankenstein*, the third of the Frankenstein films in which he played the monster. He used to see his daughter frequently when he lived in New York after leaving Hollywood. Sara is now married

and has a family of her own. Boris Karloff and Dorothy
Stine were divorced in 1945. According to the *Picture
Show* files at the British Film Institute, I discovered
that there had been an earlier marriage to a dancer,
Polly, which had also ended in divorce. This marriage is
not mentioned in any of the usual film reference-books
and Karloff himself never referred to it. In fact Polly
was the professional name of Helene Vivian Soule
whom Karloff married in 1923.

An account was published in the American *Movie
Classics* in 1932 stating that a former wife of Clark
Gable had a young and pretty woman call on her one
day; a woman who gave her name as Pauline Karloff.
She said she was being pestered by reporters to tell
them sensational stories about her former husband,
Boris Karloff, and she wanted some advice. She had
been divorced from Karloff in 1929 and had been making
her living painting portraits in an original way and
renting her work to film studios using modern settings.
Often there were times when she did not know where
her next meal was coming from but when a big Sunday
newspaper offered her a large sum of money for a
personally signed story about Boris she refused, and
when the offer was doubled, she still refused. 'As an
artist,' she is reported to have said, 'I wish success to a
fellow artist . . . but why drag me into this? I have been
out of his life for three years now. When we meet on
the Boulevard we don't speak.'

An announcement in *The Times* of 2nd May 1946, that
Karloff had married Evelyn Helmore (nee Hope) in
California was almost the first news of the marriage that
had taken place at Las Vegas, Nevada, on 11th April

1946. Many of the Hollywood publicity men seem to have missed it, although it did cause something of a stir, Mrs Karloff told me. Then again, it was a quiet wedding but usually, in America, that is the signal for more photographs and press coverage than otherwise!

Evelyn Hope Helmore, an Englishwoman who came from Putney, had known Karloff for some years before they were married; she met him in Hollywood where she was assistant story-editor to Darryl F Zanuck. And although she had never been connected with the production of any of Karloff's films, she told me she had sometimes worked on the same lot with him. In 1951, the Karloffs moved to a luxurious apartment in New York where they discovered that they could be 'home' in London overnight by air! This had not occurred to them when living in California where they had a beautiful house and garden where they spent a lot of time, but now from New York they began to fly over to England every summer and it wasn't long before they both decided that England was the place where they wanted to settle. This took some organising, but finally everything was arranged and they returned home.

It was 1959 when the Karloffs finally moved to England, and in 1960 Boris Karloff joined the exclusive Garrick Club, named after actor and dramatist, David Garrick, and still today full of the atmosphere of the stage with its mementos and six hundred theatrical portraits; and it was at the Garrick Club that the late W Macqueen Pope (the beloved 'Popey') told me of Karloff's kindness in helping to launch his book on the history of Drury Lane Theatre. This theatre is associated with the most famous of all theatre ghosts – the 'Man in Grey' – and the visitors who went to look for the ghost on that occasion included, apart from Karloff and 'Popey', the great character actor Tod Slaughter, who gained his reputation in such melodramas as *Sweeney Todd* and *The Murder in the Red Barn*. Slaughter also told me about this memorable visit to Drury Lane Theatre in the company of the Frankenstein 'monster', and, I recall, presented me with a portrait inscribed: *From the Devil himself, Tod Slaughter*! Others present were Valentine Dyall, the deep-voiced broadcaster of the *Man in Black* series and ex-Superintendent Bob Fabian of Scotland Yard. Boris Karloff told me in June 1967 that they all had drinks and heard about the ghost and that was about it. 'Popey' loved to tell people about the ghost of Drury Lane and he told me that he had seen the mysterious figure not once, but several times, and always in daylight. Fred Archer, former editor of *Psychic News* mentions the visit in his chronicle of psychic experiences, *Ghost Writer* (1966).

Mr and Mrs Boris Karloff always lived a very private life and he was quite embarrassed when he was the subject of a *This is Your Life* programme in America. They did a lot of research for the programme, but came up with some awful 'bloomers', such as an ornate door-knob with personal associations, whereas the actual one had been a very ordinary, wooden one, Mrs Karloff told me.

This is of necessity a short chapter. Very little was generally known of the private life of Boris Karloff; just about as much in fact as he chose to make public. Perhaps this is not a bad thing. His acting and film appearances constituted his life-work and although inevitably he was a famous figure and everything about him of interest to the public, his private life always remained very private, and I for one hesitated to intrude on that last stronghold of someone of the calibre of Boris Karloff who, because of his work in films and television and on stage and radio, was so often in the public eye. One might indeed wish that all other actors and actresses were as particular regarding their private lives. I remember very well a typical answer to one of my requests for impressions and opinions on the actor and the man from people who had met or knew him . . . This came from J B Priestley: 'I wish I could help you about Karloff, but I only met him very briefly and he seemed to me then a very pleasant, intelligent actor, remarkably different from the various monsters he has played in Hollywood.'

Towards the end of his life, Karloff wore a metal brace on one leg. 'I can't breathe and I can't walk,' he used to joke. 'Must be the result of carrying too many bodies upstairs!' He had suffered with bronchitis in California and he'd had an arthritic knee for years. But still his sporting interests continued, and he loved to follow cricket and rugger matches, both in Britain and in America. He was a Lord's Taverner and belonged to Middlesex and Surrey Cricket Clubs, and to the end of his life he watched matches whenever he could – sometimes when he shouldn't!

I asked him once about film directing. 'I've never had the opportunity', he replied, 'and it's too late now; and there is nothing I would rather *not* do. There is always somebody breathing down the back of your neck from "front office" – the backers.' . . . 'Everything in the film industry is a crisis,' Karloff continued and went on to tell me about an incident during the making of *The Raven*, in 1962, when he had asked for advice on one particular point and had been told to do it any way he liked!

It is no secret that playwrights and other writers were always Karloff's natural friends, for it was with other people with lively minds that he was most happy. Such a man is Robert Bloch whom I met at a literary function in London a year or two ago and I talked to him about Karloff. Robert Bloch is the author of the successful thriller *Psycho*; he met Karloff many times and they became good friends. One of the phrases that has always stuck in Robert Bloch's memory is Karloff saying: 'A monster's life is not a happy one'; although I think that he was primarily thinking of the hours and hours of torturing time taken to apply and remove the arduous make-up for his monster roles. When the Frankestein films were shot the rest of the cast assembled at eight o'clock in the morning but by then Karloff had been at the studio for more than three hours, having his make-up applied; and when he played the early scenes of *The Mummy*, it was a four hour make-up job. All the same Karloff enjoyed these monster roles and he deplored some of the poor 'quickies' that were churned out later that degraded the field of horror pictures, or as Karloff *would* have it, terror films. As I left him, Robert Bloch reassured me on one point: 'Oh, yes' he said, 'Boris is the happiest monster I've met!'

Fritz Lang, the great writer-director of such films as *Metropolis*, *Nibelung Saga*, *Doctor Mabuse* and *M*, met

Karloff at a dinner party given by Bob and Ellie Bloch and the two old-timers got along famously. Lang said afterwards, 'I liked Karloff enormously.' They referred to each other throughout the evening as the two 'old dinosaurs'. Fritz Lang, up early as always, saw the news-flash about Karloff's death on American television and broke the news to Robert Bloch and a number of other Americans.

Karloff was forced into a strange role in his acting career and not allowed to leave it, and his professional life might be compared with that fine actor, William Penley, who played Babbs in *Charley's Aunt* so well that he found himself still playing the part twenty years later! But Karloff kept himself intact; given a little more self-love (and he was completely without pride of self), and a touch of ham, Karloff, after thirty odd years as a monster – as Samuel Grafton once pointed out – might have become a bit of a Hollywood zombie himself! In fact, he remained exactly as he had been at the beginning. It was, perhaps, his greatest accomplishment.

As is so often the case with players who specialise in a certain type of part, the actual character of the man was very different from that which he portrayed on the screen. He was quiet, gentle and reserved, with a fundamental sense of pathos which he could not always hide, and perhaps this contributed to his success – for it added a further dimension to parts that were never subtly conceived, and he will be remembered as an actor who understood the visual requirements of the cinema and could play a horrific part with restraint, even a delicacy, which modern productions so often lack.

CHAPTER 8

Films, Films . . .

SOME IDEA OF the enormous industry that film-making had become in the mid 'thirties can be glimpsed from Beth Day's description of the Hollywood property department, in her book *This Was Hollywood* (1960). Something like 350,000 articles that ranged from 1,800 genuine antiques (many were imported from Europe for films like *Romeo and Juliet* and *A Tale of Two Cities*) were contained in the inventory, which included glassware of all periods; a collection of American and Continental telephones; a 'paper' room that contained stamps, telephone directories – and the family mortgage! There was a locked arsenal with authentic firearms ranging from frontier to modern weapons, and a 'rubber' room which could, and did, convert an Indian elephant into an African one by fitting larger ears!

In the middle of this hive of industry in 1935, Karloff starred in Columbia's *The Black Room*, directed by Roy William Neill, with Marian Marsh and Robert Allen; a period melodrama based on the Hungarian legend that the family of Berghmanns began with twin sons. The elder son was said to have been murdered by the younger and it was believed that the family would end when history repeated itself. In the dual-role, Karloff differentiated admirably between the two brothers and was equally effective as villain and hero. Elaborate settings and good photography helped to make this picture successful and had the film had better dialogue and more subtle direction, it would have been an even more outstanding thriller. In 1936 Karloff referred to *The Black Room* as 'my favourite picture so far.'

Ever since the phenomenal success of *Frankenstein*, four years earlier, Universal and James Whale knew they had been premature in destroying the monster in the blazing mill at the end of the film and they had been searching for a worthy sequel. They almost achieved this with *The Bride of Frankenstein* (1935) with its similar theme – although some people found the film morbid: film-critic Ernest Betts of the *Sunday Express* described the film as an 'unpleasant shocker' which 'revels in its morbidity'. Ever-practical, *The Times* asked how the bride knew, at the moment of her artificial creation, the significance of the lever, the sole purpose of which, it seemed, was to blow the laboratory and everything in it skyhigh?

Originally, *Frankenstein* had had a happy ending with Baron Frankenstein (Frederick Kerr) toasting the health and happiness of his son. In 1935, Universal had the last scene excised from circulating prints so that the film closed with the blazing mill and the happy ending was almost forgotten in Universal's vaults, until *Franken-stein* was released for American television in 1957, when the original ending was restored. For the sequel, script-writers William Hurlbut and John L Balderston had the monster fall to the mill's flooded cellar and so escape both the flames and the mob of angry villagers.

The technical side of *Bride of Frankenstein* was extraordinarily good, and the eerie nature of some of the episodes was emphasised by the excellence of the acting. Boris Karloff (included in the cast as 'Karloff') headed a strong list of actors, including Colin Clive (again playing Doctor Frankenstein); Elsa Lanchester as the twitchy, bird-like moving, bride created for the monster – the ancient Egyptian Queen Nefertiti was used as 'model'; Ernest Thesiger as the sinister necromancer, scientist and grave-robber Dr Praetorius, and Valerie Hobson as Mrs Frankenstein who is abducted by the monster.

Elsa Lanchester in her white shroud and Karloff in his weird make-up enact a brief but memorable courtship, wherein there is a delicate suggestion of both the wedding bed and the grave. One of the girls who was a 'stand-in' for Elsa Lanchester in this film nearly lost her reason. Trussed up like a guineafowl and under strict orders not to make a sound, she had a sudden and overwhelming attack of claustrophobia. Screaming, she upset the rest of the actors and technicians on the set, all of whom suffered abnormal nerve strain. Elsa Lanchester herself found the experience of being encased from head to foot in about two miles of linen – like a living mummy – terrifying, and for the three days that were required to shoot the bride scenes, she more or less lived in a cataleptic trance, propped up on the set like an enbalmed body or lying gracefully in a coffin, unable to talk or move! She even had to be fed by her dresser or studio friends as her hands were heavily bandaged right down to the fingertips.

Writing about the Frankenstein films in *Films and*

Filming in 1957, Karloff said: '. . . I had to portray a sub-human of little intelligence and without speech, still getting over the sympathetic qualities in the role. When the monster did speak (in the second film) I knew that this was eventually going to destroy the character. It did for me anyway. I believe the British Censor cut a scene from *Bride of Frankenstein* because of what he thought in his own mind were necrophile tendencies. I must say that I have never knowingly been in a scene that was objectionable to good taste. Some of my films have been stupid and silly, because they did not have good stories; but they have never been distasteful.' *Bride of Frankenstein* was publicised in the British film trade as 'for adults only and quite unsuitable for children or for nervous people of any age.' Carlos Clarens has suggested that with *King Kong*, *Bride of Frankenstein* remains Hollywood's finest moment of unbridled imagination.

The commercial success of *House of Doom*, prompted the studios to reunite Karloff and Lugosi, and Universal turned to the pen of Edgar Allan Poe and produced *The Raven* (1935) directed by Louis Friedlander (later Lew Landers). The film was a combination of two of Poe's *Tales of Mystery and Imagination* woven into a story of a mad scientist who, for a hobby, reconstructs in stone and iron, and equips with the instruments of torture, the dungeons imagined by Edgar Allan Poe. Finally, under emotional stress, he becomes obsessed into using them. With Bela Lugosi, Irene Ware and Lester Matthews the acting in the film was excellent and the technical side of a very high order, but there was perhaps too much of Poe's horror and not enough of his imagination. Karloff himself thought the film was a mistake.

'Here was an attempt,' he said, 'to pile on the thrills without much logic.' But even in this picture there was a certain amount of sympathy for the unfortunate central character – an essential for a successful thriller. Lugosi was the sadistic scientist, influenced by the writings of Edgar Allan Poe, who builds the torture chamber suggested in *The Pit and the Pendulum.* He changes escaped-murderer Karloff's face by making one side hideous and then offers to change it back, if Karloff will help him seduce Irene Ware and torture her father, Samuel S Hinds. Instead, Karloff saves both father and daughter and kills Lugosi in one of the torture devices. Referring to the use of two live ravens in the 1963 horror-comic remake of the film, Karloff told me the original version was simplicity itself: 'Why, it was nothing but a bloody stuffed bird on Bela Lugosi's desk!'

From this film onwards Lugosi's screen roles were subservient to Karloff's when they appeared in pictures together, and the style was set as Universal continued to cash in on the popularity of horror pictures during the 'thirties, and on Karloff's portrayal of monsters and mad scientists by starring the two actors in *The Invisible Ray* (1936). This spectacular and fantastic thriller of the horrific type was skillfully directed by Lambert Hillyer and set in Paris and wildest Africa. It concerned a scientist who discovered a substance far more powerful than radium which both healed and destroyed. Having absorbed a deadly dose himself, his mere touch meant instant death. The scientist is gradually driven mad and ultimately killed. Brilliant direction and camera-work (by George Robinson and John P Fulton) helped to make *The Invisible Ray* a memorable film. Lugosi, in his third film with Karloff played the good-hearted man while Karloff was the sinister Dr Rukh, who, after killing Lugosi, went up in flames himself. For his fine work on *The Invisible Ray*, Lambert Hillyer was rewarded with the direction of *Dracula's Daughter*, the long-awaited sequel to the original *Dracula* and based on Bram Stoker's story *Dracula's Guest*. The cast included Gloria Holden, Otto Kruger, Edward Van Sloan, Claud Alister and E E Clive in addition to Lugosi as the sinister Count Dracula.

That year of 1936 also saw Boris Karloff with Ricardo Cortez and Edmund Gwenn in a tense drama of a man brought back to life after being electrocuted, aptly entitled *The Walking Dead* (Warner Brothers). It was the first of many films with a similar theme: Karloff is brought back to life after being electrocuted for a crime he did not commit and sets out on an avenging spree to kill all his enemies. When his self-appointed task is completed, life once more leaves his body. Karloff played the role in a low key and was quietly effective in a strangely disquieting film.

Karloff next appeared in *Charlie Chan at the Opera* (20th-Century Fox) directed by H Bruce Humberstone, one of the original series of films depicting the entertaining, inscrutable and Confucius-quoting Chinese detective, played by Warner Oland, an actor of talent who died two years later at the age of 57. Karloff had the part of a demented singer, a murder suspect, in what has been described as 'one of the best of the Chan series.'

By now, Karloff was exercising discretion in his choice of roles and in the manner in which he played them, and he began to build a reputation for reliable versatility and wisely included non-horror films when the roles suited him. Two films were made in Britain at this time, and while exploring Karloff's acting ability in credible circumstances they provided plenty of thrills without descending to horrific sensationalism.

The Man Who Changed His Mind (Gaumont-British, 1935) directed by Robert Stevenson, presented Karloff as a scientist who had discovered a method of transferring the mind 'contact' of the human brain from one person to that of another. Anna Lee, John Loder and Frank Cellier ably assisted Karloff in a well written story and finely directed film. In case the story sounds too gentle for a Karloff film perhaps I should add that Karloff was a revengeful scientist who transplants the brains from cripples to men he thinks have wronged him! Donald Calthrop gave a memorable study of a paralytic.

The second British film was *Juggernaut* (J H Productions, 1936), and saw Karloff in an excellent thriller set in the Riviera. The film was competently directed by Henry Edwards and the story, although improbable, was well acted and the film contained plenty of action, Karloff being his usual sinister self in a black homburg and morning dress, ably supported by Joan Wyndham, Arthur Margetson and Gibb McLaughlin. *Juggernaut* was made at Twickenham during Karloff's second visit to England in twenty-seven years. As Rachael Low has pointed out in *The History of the British Film 1914–1918* (1950), it was 'not until London Films Company was established in 1913 in the converted skating-rink at St Margaret's, Twickenham, that the Art Direction of

British film production was taken seriously. Under Dr Jubb, the managing director, a standard of detail and finish was achieved which surpassed even the best American efforts.' Before the disastrous fire in 1918, Twickenham studios (when owned by London Films Company in 1916) was the largest studio in the country and could take as many as eight sets at once. Twickenham film studios, where Josef von Sternberg had once been a three-pound a week assistant director, had not been used for first feature films for a good many years, until such films as *Zulu* and *A Hard Day's Night* brought these famous studios back into full use. Visiting Twickenham Studios in 1962, I was introduced by Guido Coen to a technician who remembered Karloff working there on *Juggernaut* some thirty years before.

Back in America, Lloyd Corrigan directed Karloff in one of his very few sympathetic roles, when the horror actor was cast as a lovable, old professor in *Night Key* (Universal, 1937), a role that appealed strongly to Karloff who was seen as a simple old inventor who discovered a burglar alarm system which was practically human. The old man was abducted by burglars who sought to control his activities, but he fooled the crooks and gave them away to the police while ostensibly working on some new electrical invention to aid them in their activities. But by this time audiences had come to expect horrors from Boris Karloff and they expressed their disappointment in no uncertain manner. *Night Key* was in fact a very capably acted and produced film; a genuine thriller which provided excitement without horror.

During the same year Karloff appeared in Warner Brothers' *West of Shanghai* (*War Lord* in America) with

Beverly Roberts and Ricardo Cortez and directed by
John Farrow. For this film Karloff adopted a painful
but effective disguise which turned him into a Chinese
bandit, but a good-hearted and high-principled man,
loyal to his friends and full of noble characteristics. The
film dealt with the contrast between his nobility and the
meanness of the Western financiers, and, while his
death was brave and saddening, the Western man's was
despicable and welcome. The acting was really excellent
and the photography good. Karloff told me this make-up
was harder to apply than the one he wore in *Frankenstein*,
but it was less uncomfortable. It may well have been
partly due to his remarkable portrayal of an oriental in
this film that the following year saw Karloff in the first
of a series of films in which he played a Chinese detective.
West of Shanghai, incidentally, was a remake, in a different
setting, of a successful film starring Leo Carrillo some
years earlier entitled *The Bad Man;* the chief character
then being a Mexican bandit.

Still with Warner Brothers Karloff made *The Invisible
Menace*, again directed by John Farrow; a murder
mystery set in the present day against the background
of the United States army and Karloff was *not* the
murderer, although he was the suspect in a series of
murders that start when a body is found pinned to the
rafters with a bayonet. The actors included Regis
Toomey, Henry Kolker and Marie Wilson and, of its
type, this was an extremely good film. It was reported
at the time that 'the standard of acting is so high that
one cannot differentiate between "stars" and "extras"
and both direction and photography are excellent, the
latter being particularly important because the action

takes place on a dark and misty night in the light of oil lamps when the electricity fails.'

William Nigh next directed Boris Karloff in the five Wong films that appeared at this time, based on Hugh Wiley's James Lee Wong stories in *Collier's Magazine*. The role of the suave and meticulous Mr Wong, specialist in criminal investigation, gave Karloff an opportunity to establish a character whose personal charm and quiet, scientific methods of detection proved a welcome change from the usual run of such films. Produced by Monogram and distributed by Pathe, Karloff appeared in 1938 with Grant Withers, Dorothy Tree, Maxine Jennings and Evelyn Brent in *Mr Wong – Detective* (entitled *Without Warning* in America); with Dorothy Tree, Grant Withers, Lotus Long, Morgan Wallace, Holmes Herbert and Craig Reynolds in *The Mystery of Mr Wong* (1939); with Grant Withers and Majorie Reynolds in *Mr Wong in Chinatown* (1939, re-issued in 1946) and with Grant Withers and Marjorie Reynolds again in *Mr Wong at Headquarters* (1940, re-issued in 1946) and *The Mystery of the 'Wentworth Castle'* (1940, reissued 1947), the latter two films being entitled *The Fatal Hour* and *Doomed to Die* respectively in America. The whole series was effectively produced and the suspense invariably well sustained.

In 1939 Karloff was back with Warner Brothers for *Devil's Island* with Nedda Harrigan and James Stephenson, directed by William Clemens, where Karloff played the part of Dr Gaudet, a medical practitioner in France who gets sent to the French Guiana penal colony for aiding a wounded, escaped prisoner. The film was made at the time when France announced that she would send no more convicts to notorious Devil's Island, and it is neither remarkable that the French government asked that changes be made by the studio in the original version of the film, nor that the film was never released in Great Britain, although it was shown here in 1969. In the film the sadistic commandant (James Stephenson) is finally exposed by his own wife (Nedda Harrigan) after Karloff saves her child's life in an operation.

Also in 1939, Karloff went back to Universal for the third and longest of the Frankenstein films, *Son of Frankenstein*, directed by Rowland V Lee, with a strong cast including Bela Lugosi, Basil Rathbone, Josephine Hutchinson and Lionel Atwill. And again Universal succeeded in making a very good film on the Frankenstein theme. Colin Clive, who had played the part of Baron Frankenstein in the two previous films, was now dead. A tradition says that it is unlucky to play this part. Colin Clive, a first-class actor, will always be remembered for his creation of the part in the first two Frankenstein films and for his rendering of Stanhope, an officer physically and mentally ravaged by war, in the 1930 stage play *Journey's End*. After *Son of Frankenstein*, the last one with Karloff as the monster, the later Frankenstein films went sadly down-hill.

Son of Frankenstein had Basil Rathbone as Baron Wolf von Frankenstein, returning to his father's castle from America with his wife and small son. There, finding that his father's monster was still alive but comatose and tended by Igor, a sinister shepherd with a broken neck (Bela Lugosi), Frankenstein is fired with enthusiasm and decides to continue his father's experiments. He succeeds in re-animating the monster, and a series of murders in the village culminate with the abduction of the Baron's son who is rescued in the nick of time, and the monster is hurled into a scalding sulphur pit. Karloff again gave a memorable portrayal as the cold-blooded monster, which this time he played without the endearing humanity of the previous films, and the monster had apparently forgotten how to talk. Lionel Atwill as the police officer was more than partially effective and Basil Rathbone gave a clever and convincing performance. Lionel Atwill died in 1946 and Basil Rathbone in 1967. The broken-necked Igor was Bela Lugosi's most outstanding characterisation after his classic role of Count Dracula.

The settings were somewhat stylised and grotesque, with a complete absence of sunlight and vegetation, but they helped to create an effective atmosphere and the production and technical quality was of a high standard. 'Psychological sets' was the term which Jack Otterson, Art Director at Universal Studios, used to describe the settings. Before the picture went into production, Otterson was given instruction to create settings which would arouse a reaction of impending danger and mystery in the mind of the beholder; yet the sets had to be in keeping with the mood of the picture. He solved the problem by departing entirely from any known style of architecture and without indulging in overstressed cubistic or surrealistic designs. 'The sets were rather an orderly array of planes and masses, which, at first glance, resembled a castle interior,' Otterson explains, 'but the angles and masses were calculated to force an impression of a weird locale without intruding too strongly into the consciousness of the spectator.'

While making this film, Karloff found a fellow lover-of-flowers in Josephine Hutchinson and it was a fantastic sight to see Karloff in his monstrous make-up and Josephine Hutchinson arrayed in the latest evening gown, drinking tea and avidly discussing petunias, roses, orchids and other flowers in moments of relaxation on the set. *Son of Frankenstein* was filmed from an original screenplay by Willis Cooper and it succeeded so well that Universal quickly followed with *Tower of London* (1939), again directed by Rowland V Lee. Karloff appeared as Mord, the grim, clubfooted and totally bald executioner. With a strong cast, including Basil Rathbone giving a magnificent performance as Richard III, Ian Hunter well portraying the brave, clever, good-humoured, but indolent Edward IV and Vincent Price and Nan Grey, this historical drama with authentic settings and fine battle scenes gave one of the best impressions of late mediaeval warfare ever to come to the screen. Taken from their context many of the later short sequences would be of great value in history teaching. I asked Ian Hunter for his impressions of Boris Karloff and this film, but he told me he and Karloff appeared in different sequences which were shot at different times, but he added: '. . . it was a pleasure to know such a charming man and a constant wonder that this fearful ogre in pictures should be so addicted to . . . cricket!'

For Columbia in 1939 Karloff appeared in *The Man They Could Not Hang*, directed by Nick Grinde, with a cast including Lorna Gray and Robert Wilcox. Karloff, the inventor of a mechanical heart which will restore life to the dead, is convicted of killing one of his students

in an experiment to bring the dead back to life. He is
condemned to the electric chair and vows he will return
and kill the judge, the district attorney and all the jurors.
Brought back to life by one of his assistants, after being
executed, he almost makes good his threats as, trapping
the judge and jurors in an empty house, he proceeds to
kill them one at a time at intervals of fifteen minutes.
Here were all the ingredients for a fine horror-thriller:
a dark and deserted house, sinister laboratories, a
macabre theme – and, of course, the menacing presence
of Boris Karloff. It is not surprising that the film provided
some hair-raising moments and Columbia followed it
with several low-budget mad-scientist thrillers, including
Behind the Door (1940) entitled *The Man With Nine Lives*
in America, with Roger Pryor and Jo Ann Sayers, a
medical mystery drama with Karloff a pioneer in the
method of curing cancer by freezing, which Nick Grinde
again directed. The film was important since it argued
the age-old case of ignorance disguised as humanitarian-
ism versus cold-blooded research which will overcome
all obstacles – including human life – in its path to
attain the truth.

CHAPTER 9

. . . and Still More Films

IN 1940 ALSO, Karloff appeared with Margaret Lindsay, Maris Wrixon, Bruce Lester, Leonard Mudie and Holmes Herbert in Warner's *Enemy Agent*, retitled *British Intelligence* in America, directed by Terry Morse; a spy drama of the Great War. Karloff, innocent of elaborate make-up, made a suitably sinister German ace spy who managed to get a job as a butler in the home of a Cabinet Minister. In the same year he appeared for Universal in *Black Friday*, directed by Arthur Lubin. At first an absent-minded professor, Karloff had· part of a gangster's brain transplanted into his skull after being accidentally run down during a car battle between gangsters. This resulted in his developing a dual-personality, being at times himself and at other times the gangster. Capable directing and an excellent performance by Karloff marked an otherwise mediocre film. During the making of this film, Arthur Lubin tells a story of Karloff and Bela Lugosi (also in the film) and both, of course, famous for their horrible make-ups – which they accepted and indeed admired on each other – meeting on the Universal set to discover that they were both working straight: that is, without make-up. Karloff, in formal morning dress was sitting on the set when Lugosi walked in wearing a plain blue suit. 'Get away! Get out!' Karloff yelled, 'I'm seeing a ghost!' 'Change your brand,' retorted Lugosi, 'It's only me and you ought to know!' 'Why ought I to know?' demanded Karloff, 'I've never seen you before in my life.' 'I've never seen you without make-up either, if it comes to that,' said Lugosi, and, turning aside to Arthur Lubin, added: 'And you can say for me that Karloff is definitely frightening!'

Bela Lugosi, the man who brought Bram Stoker's famous vampire story *Dracula* (1930) to the screen had a tragic life. He made £200,000 from *Dracula*, playing the four-hundred-year-old Count in films and on the stage in America and Europe for three years, but during the latter part of his life (he died in 1956), he became a drug addict and an alcoholic; his money, his voice and his magnetic personality were all gone. In accordance with a last request the seventy-five-year-old actor was buried in 'Dracula's' black cloak with its red lining, that he so loved.

Karloff next went to RKO Radio for *You'll Find Out* (released in 1941), directed by David Butler with Peter Lorre, Bela Lugosi, Helen Parrish and starring Kay Kyser and his Band – a mystery with music and comedy. On the night following one of the regular Wednesday broadcasts, Kay Kyser and his Band play for James Ballacrest's twenty-first birthday party at Ballacrest Manor, an eerie, gloomy mansion. James is an orphan whose Aunt Margo inherited the estate and has been trying to get in touch with her brother through a spurious medium. Kay and the boys become suspicious and decide to see what they can find out about the mysterious house. They find several sliding panels and secret passages that lead them to the 'medium's' workshop, where they discover the paraphernalia for his fraudulent séances. At the next séance Kay exposes the trickery and the 'medium' and his accomplice are caught in their own net and blown to pieces. Altogether, the film was a happy mixture of creeps and joke situations with some interesting trick photography and sound effects. Kay Kyser and his Band produced some excellent musical numbers and a good deal of comedy, and Boris Karloff, Peter Lorre and Bela Lugosi suitably dampened their spirits in their usual eerie roles. Karloff was later to act with Peter Lorre in *The Bogie Man Will get You* (1943), *The Raven* (1962), *The Terror* (1963) and *Comedy of Terrors* (1963); he was to say after Lorre's death: 'He was a delightful man; I miss Peter terribly. A truly original actor: there was no one like him.'

In 1940 Karloff had appeared in *Before I Hang* (Columbia), directed by Nick Grinde, with Evelyn Keys and Bruce Bennett. This was a scientific melodrama in which Dr John Garth (played by Boris Karloff), an elderly scientist, in attempting to prove that he has discovered a cure for death, kills an aged pauper. For this the doctor is sentenced to be hanged, but while awaiting execution he becomes friendly with the prison surgeon and the two men continue Garth's experiments in the prison laboratory. The day before he is to be hanged Dr Garth is injected with a serum made from the blood of a murderer who has paid the price for his crimes. Immediately following the injection Dr Garth is granted a reprieve and later pardoned but the serum, though it succeeds in making him younger, also turns him into a murderer and he strangles four people before being shot by a police officer. A gruesome and fantastic film that contained no relief of any kind to lighten the heaviness of the plot; it was however, competently directed and enabled Karloff to give a spine-chilling performance as the demented scientist.

The Ape directed by William Nigh, was released in 1941; a horrific thriller, with Karloff as the half-mad doctor who believes he has discovered a cure for paralysis in a serum from the spinal cord of a human being. Killing an ape that breaks into his laboratory, the doctor uses its skin as a disguise when he sets out to find more liquid for the serum. On one of his forays he is shot by the police and mortally wounded, but as he dies he sees his patient rise from her chair and falter towards him and he knows that the serum has worked. Maris Wrixon shared the acting honours with Karloff in this Monogram film distributed by Pathe.

Back at Columbia, Karloff appeared in *The Devil Commands* (1941) directed by Edward Dmytryk, a serious drama with Karloff as a respectable scientist who has perfected an apparatus to register brain reaction. His wife is killed in a car smash just after he has recorded her brain impulses, and Karloff, half-demented with grief, determines to try to communicate with her spirit through the brain machine. He hires a spiritualist medium to work with him, but after his janitor loses some of his faculties following a disastrous experiment they are forced to go into hiding. One day the housekeeper is killed while spying on them, and Karloff accidentally kills the medium and forces his daughter to help him.

At the critical moment, the enraged villagers storm the house, the apparatus explodes and Karloff is killed. It is interesting to notice that the Second World War, then at its height, with its many inevitable bereavements, induced a spate of novels, plays and films dealing with the possibility of communication with the departed. *The Devil Commands* was a well-made film and Karloff was very convincing in the varied aspects of the character he depicted without resorting to weird make-up. At last, it seemed, producers were using to advantage the hidden menace in the velvety tones of that remarkable voice.

1943 saw Karloff in *The Bogie Man Will Get You* (Columbia), directed by Lew Landers, with Peter Lorre. This comedy-horror film with Karloff as Professor Nathaniel Billings who is conducting experiments to turn ordinary men into supermen, has an escaped Fascist who throws a bomb which helps to wake things up, and in the end the police march the entire bunch off to the asylum! Through it all, both Karloff and Peter Lorre well sustained the appearance of mental unbalance; but what a waste of talent.

Karloff next appeared in the Technicolor Universal film *The Climax* (1944), directed by George Waggner with Susanna Foster and Turhan Bey. Madly in love with a beautiful opera star, Marcellina, and jealous of her career, Dr Hohner (Karloff) strangles her. The truth of her strange disappearance is never known and he is pitied for his obvious heartbreak. Ten years later he hears a voice strangely like hers and finds two music students, Franz and Angela, practising. The girl makes an instant success and the doctor is determined that *her* lovely voice shall be kept from the public too. He uses his professional position at the State Theatre to examine her throat, and hypnotises her in order to gain control of her mind. He suggests to her that she does not want to sing any more and to the dismay of Franz, her lover, and to the joy of Jarmila, the established star, she breaks down. Dr Hohner takes her to his house, ostensibly for treatment, but really to gain entire power over her. Franz suspects him and he is aided by Louise, the house-keeper, once Marcellina's maid. Franz manages to inveigle the very young king into issuing a royal com-mand that Angela shall sing before him, and on the appointed night the two powers of love and hate fight for Angela's voice. Foiled in the end, the doctor returns to an underground room where he has kept the embalmed body of his dead wife in a glass coffin, and as the police rush towards him a lighted bowl overturns and he is burnt to death as the draperies swiftly catch fire . . . 'Boris Karloff sustained the main part excellently, his frozen face and quiet voice being full of maniac posses-sion', said a current trade paper. This was Karloff's first colour film and the sets were those created for the 1943 remake of *The Phantom of the Opera*.

The Body Snatchers (RKO Radio) was directed by Robert Wise and released in 1945. Karloff gave one of his best personations with Bela Lugosi and Henry Daniel (who gave a brilliant performance) in the macabre Robert Louis Stevenson story set in Edinburgh in 1832. The grim atmosphere surrounding the pest of grave-robbing to supply bodies for scientific purposes was well maintained throughout the film. There was an excellent scene in which a little flower-seller is to be murdered by Karloff.

The girl wanders away down a foggy street, singing quietly to herself as Karloff follows in a carriage, the horse clip-clopping over the cobbles. The camera keeps its position until the girl and the carriage have disappeared in the fog and then the girl's singing, now very faint, suddenly breaks off – and the scene fades out. In *The Film Till Now*, Paul Rotha refers to this film as 'almost certainly the superior of all horror films, at least in terms of literacy and mature approach.' The film was produced by Val Lewton, a former sub-editor for David O Selznick, and his precisely constructed and neatly executed horror films achieved a vogue among the intellectuals – particularly *The Cat People* (1942) and *I Walked With a Zombie* (1943), with its intense and compelling atmosphere which has rarely been equalled, while *Youth Runs Wild* (1944) is usually considered to be the best of the 'city streets' school of films about juvenile delinquency in wartime. The film was made in 1943, but was not released until 1945 so it did not clash with other Val Lewton films. *The Body Snatchers* was the first of the three good horror films Karloff made with the Val Lewton unit. Val Lewton died in 1951 from a heart attack at the early age of forty-six.

In the same year, Karloff appeared with Ellen Drew and Marc Cramer in RKO's *The Isle of the Dead*, directed by Mark Robson and produced by Val Lewton, a tale of evil spirits abroad during the confinement of a group of people on an island off the Greek mainland during the Baltic war of 1812 ('as brutally frightening and gratifying a horror film as I can remember,' said James Agee); and in the Universal thriller *House of Frankenstein*, directed by Erle C Kenton. In this film Karloff had the part of Dr Gustov Neuman – a mad scientist who escapes from prison, where he has been incarcerated for fifteen years because of his experiments in black magic, accompanied by a hump-backed murderer. They kill the owner and driver of a travelling Chamber of Horrors show and with it they continue their journey, Dr Neuman wishing to revenge himself on the three men who had him imprisoned. The doctor brings back to life Count Dracula (John Carradine) whose skeleton, complete with stake through it, had been obtained by the showman (George Zucco) together with earth from Transylvania, and the vampire assists him in his mission of vengeance. This film contained memorable scenes of the transformation from human form to that of a vampire bat. The Count is finally destroyed by his exposure to the rays of the early morning sun before he can reach the haven of his earth-filled coffin. Dr Neuman having found and killed his enemies, is accompanied by his murderer friend, and a gypsy dancing-girl they have rescued from a cruel master. They eventually arrive at Frankenstein's revived laboratory, where they restore to life Larry Talbot, the Wolfman, from his tomb of ice. Dr Neuman then turns his attention to restoring the Frankenstein monster. The gypsy girl falls in love with Talbot, but he becomes once more a werewolf and is shot by her with a silver bullet ('someone who loves him enough to understand'): only then will he find eternal rest. The resurrected monster and Dr Neuman are pursued by villagers as they flee and eventually perish in a quagmire. Against the highly theatrical background and among the bizarre creatures he has restored to life Karloff seemed oddly out of place, and almost humble, as Dr Neuman –

and distinctly unenthusiastic as he and the apathetic-looking monster force themselves into the quagmire at the end. Glenn Strange, an ex-wrestler, had the stamina to wear the cumbersome monster make-up in this, the last but one Frankenstein film in which Karloff appeared.

Karloff next appeared in *Bedlam* (1946) for RKO, an interesting and unusual film which suffered from a weak script. It portrayed the infamous eighteenth century London asylum, where the inmates were treated as beasts by the sadistic keeper (Karloff) who confines a perfectly sane girl (Anna Lee). She eventually brings the scandalous affair to light. This, Val Lewton's last film, was not released in Britain, but has been shown at the National Film Theatre, London. *The Man Who Dared* followed from Columbia the same year, directed by John Sturges, and concerned a newspaper columnist, Don Wayne, played by George Macready, who was once responsible for the conviction of an innocent man on circumstantial grounds. He allows himself to be convicted for a murder in which he has become involved, also on circumstantial evidence alone, so that he can prove its insufficiency. His friend, who has proof of Wayne's innocence ready for production at the right time, is robbed and severely injured by the real murderer, played by Boris Karloff. Wayne manages to escape from prison and surmounts dangers and difficulties before proving his innocence and the truth of his story. Well directed and excellently acted, the film was praised for having a far more worthwhile theme than most thrillers.

Another thriller, *Personal Column* (United Artists, 1947), entitled *Lured* in America, was directed by

Douglas Sirk and Karloff appeared with George Sanders, Charles Coburn, Lucille Ball and Sir Cedric Hardwicke. This strong cast saved the film by excellent acting in a story of a homicidal maniac who made a speciality of killing young girls, and in order to do so made assignations with them through the Personal Columns of newspapers. After each murder he sent verses to Scotland Yard which contained some sort of clue and at length a friend of the latest victim is persuaded to act as a decoy. She replies to likely advertisements and after vain and unpleasant experiences with bad characters, none of whom is the one she seeks, she falls in love with a man who is not the guilty party either, but for whom she almost succeeds in procuring a conviction on circumstantial evidence. Eventually, of course, the real criminal is brought to book. Karloff played a demented clothes designer, a suspect, but not the murderer. Thought by some critics to be unnecessarily long, the film enabled its cast to produce vivid characterisations. The film was a remake of the French *Pieges* (1939), which Robert Siodmak directed with Maurice Chevalier and Erich von Stroheim as the stars, the latter in the role Karloff played.

Also in 1947, Karloff appeared in two outstanding films: *Unconquered* and *The Secret Life of Walter Mitty*. *Unconquered* with Paulette Goddard, Gary Cooper and Howard Da Silva was a Cecil B De Mille spectacular and cost close to $4,000,000. It took two years of research; one hundred days to film and brought to the sets a cast of principal and supporting players whose combined salaries exceeded one million dollars – the largest outlay for talent for a single film in De Mille's thirty-four years as a producer and director, up to that

time. *Unconquered* (Paramount) told 'in glorious Technicolor' a chapter of American history: the story of the year
1763 when Pontiac, chief of the Ottawas, led eighteen
Indian nations in a final desperate struggle to halt the
white man's march westward. After burning forts and
massacring settlements along five hundred miles of the
frontier, the Indians were finally defeated at Fort Pitt
after a ninety-day seige. Karloff played the part of
Guyasuta, longhaired Chief of the Senecas, and added to
the colour of the film with vivid saxe-blue stripes across
his naked chest! *The Secret Life of Walter Mitty*, directed
by Norman Z McLeod for RKO Radio, saw Karloff
among a cast that included Danny Kaye, Virginia
Mayo and Fay Bainter in a film that was simply a superb
comedy vehicle for the exuberant genius of Danny Kaye.
In the same year Karloff appeared as Gruesome, a
gangster who is killed after his gang rob a bank in
Dick Tracy Meets Gruesome, also for RKO.

The following year, Karloff was with Universal-
International for *Tap Roots*, directed by George Marshall.
With a big cast including Van Heflin, Susan Hayward,
Julie London, Ward Bond and Whitfield Connor, this
Technicolor period melodrama depicted the adventures
of the inhabitants of the Dabney farm in Lebanon
County who decided to remain neutral when Mississipi
withdrew from the Union. It was a competent and
colourful epic with good photography making the most of
some spirited battle scenes. Karloff, however, appeared
to be miscast as a friendly and educated Choctaw Indian.

Back to comedy in 1949 Karloff appeared in *Abbott
and Costello Meet the Killer, Boris Karloff* for Universal-
International, directed by Charles T Barton, with the

irrepressible Bud Abbott and Lou Costello making all
the necessary facial expressions and smart wisecracks and
Karloff trying to keep a straight face through it all.
Four years later he was again teamed with them in
Abbott and Costello Meet Dr Jekyll and Mr Hyde directed by
Charles Lamont. This film drew from the *Monthly Film
Bulletin* critic the comment: 'Boris Karloff is superior
to his surroundings.'

In 1951, Karloff appeared in *The Strange Door*,
directed by Joseph Pevney, with Charles Laughton and
Sally Forrest. It was the story of an evil uncle plotting
to marry his niece to a malignant libertine, a poor
adaptation of the Robert Louis Stevenson's story
The Sire de Maletroit's Door.

Then in 1952, he played in *The Black Castle*, directed
by Nathan Juran and produced by William Allard.
Karloff played alongside Richard Greene, Stephen
MacNally, Paula Corday and Lon Chaney Jnr. Jerry
Sackheim's story and screenplay, set in the eighteenth
century, centres on the castle of a sinister Austrian
count (Stephen McNally) who plots hideous deaths for
his enemies. A young adventurer, Sir Ronald Burton
(Richard Greene) believes his two friends have been
killed by the Count and gains admittance to the Black
Castle by assuming a false name; there he meets the
Count's beautiful and unwilling, young wife (Paula
Corday). Her only friend is Dr Meisser (Boris Karloff),
a medical man kept in bondage by the Count. After Sir
Ronald uncovers evidence that convinces him that the
Count is indeed responsible for the murder of his friends,
he decides to go to the Austrian emperor. As soon as he
leaves the castle the Count, who has discovered that his
wife is in love with the handsome Sir Ronald, throws

her into a dungeon and makes plans to murder her. Dr Meisser overtakes Sir Ronald, tells him what has happened and they return to the castle where Sir Ronald is promptly imprisoned himself. Dr Meisser tells Sir Ronald and the Count's wife that he can save them by giving them a drug which makes them appear dead for ten hours. He will arrange to have them buried and then dig them up. They agree, but the Count does not believe that they have taken poison and forces Dr Meisser to reveal the truth. The Count decides that burial alive is a fitting death and the ten hours are just up as the Count visits the graveyard. As he lifts the coffin-lid for a final look, he is confronted by a pair of duelling pistols which Dr Meisser has slipped into Sir Ronald's hands before clamping down the lid. Sir Ronald blazes away and the Count is killed.

Karloff was seen on the cinema screen in the following year as Colonel March, the one-eyed police investigator bringing three miscreants to justice in *Colonel March Investigates* (Criterion Films), a three-in-one story by Carter Dickson (John Dickson Carr, the brilliant detective story writer) for the lively Hyams Brothers, directed by Cyril Endfield with Joan Sims, Dana Wynter, Ewan Roberts and Sheila Burrell. Karloff created the character of Colonel March from the Department of Queer Complaints on British television; he described the role to me as a 'sympathetic part with overtures.' In the same year, Karloff appeared in the Italian film *Il Mostro dell'Isola* (*The Monster of the Island*), directed by Roberto Montero with Renato Vicario, Franca Marzi and Jole Fierro; and again in *Sabaka* (also known as *The Hindu*), directed by Frank

Farrin. This film was made partly in India, the cast including Nino Marcel, Lou Krugman, Reginald Denny and Victor Jory. Karloff appeared in three short sequences, and, although his raised eyebrows and sinister sideways glances added much-needed atmosphere to a complicated story involving a forest fire and worshippers of Sabaka (the Fire Demon), devil worship and a pet elephant and tiger, the film was only moderately successful.

In *Voodoo Island* (Bel Air Productions, 1956), directed by Reginald Le Borg, with Beverly Tyler, Karloff played a straight part in this strange tale about an expedition being attacked by carnivorous plants and suffering from zombie-like trances on a tropical island. In 1957 Karloff's voice was heard providing the commentary in an Italian six-minute Technicolor cartoon *The Juggler of Our Lady* (produced by Paul Terry for 20th-Century Fox in Cinemascope). The following year he appeared in *Frankenstein 1970*, directed by Howard W Koch for Allied Artists, with Jana Lund and Don Barry. This film was an ill-conceived attempt in cinemascope to mix the Frankenstein monster with hypnotism and atomic steam. Karloff played Baron Victor von Frankenstein, great-grandson of the creator of the original monster.

In 1958, Boris Karloff also appeared in the good, British-made Eros film *Grip of the Strangler*, directed by Robert Day with Jean Kent, Elizabeth Allen and Tim Turner. Set in Newgate prison and concerning a public execution which is investigated by a criminologist (played by Boris Karloff) the trail ends at the grave of the executed man, Karloff himself having committed the crime in a secondary personality. Also that same year, Karloff made *Corridors of Blood* for MGM, again produced in Britain, with Betta St John, Adrienne Corri, Christopher Lee and Finlay Currie. Robert Day once more directed. Previously announced under the titles of *The Doctor from Seven Dials* and *Corridors of Death*, Metro-Goldwyn-Mayer Pictures informed me on 26th June 1962 that the film had been completed and the title of *Corridors of Blood* would stay: the film was released towards the end of the year and concerned body-snatching and the early days of anaesthetics.

Now the time had come for Hollywood to mock at its own monsters, and in 1962 Karloff appeared in horror-comedy. *The Raven*, a spoof on the Edgar Allan Poe stories, was crazy but surprisingly funny. For director Roger Corman, this was his first horror-comic after some of the most stylistic horror films in years. Richard Matheson, the film-writer who scripted *The Raven* and its follow-up *Comedy of Terrors*, once said, 'with horror, you always throw them off balance. They're not just ripe for a laugh, they're *desperate* for one!' Of *The Raven*, the *Financial Times* had this to say: 'The romping of two rival magicians and the constant exhumation of mouldering corpses eventually got tedious. The compensations are occasional moments of high comedy in the florid decoration of it all and in the masterly send-up of Basil Rathbone, Peter Lorre and the sibilant Boris Karloff.' Karloff spoke of Corman, one of the most prolific commercial film-makers of his time, as 'inspiring as a director and with a distinct Gothic sense . . .' when I talked to him about *The Raven* which was completed in sixteen days and three days ahead of schedule! In

Horror Movies, Carlos Clarens recounts that when Corman found some sets standing and Karloff on his hands, he decided it was a pity to waste the sets, not to mention the valuable services of Boris Karloff, so he and two screen-writers hastily concocted a storyline, incorporating some fine seascape scenes shot at Monterey, California, by Corman's assistant, Monte Hellman; and they completed *The Terror*, a confusing, but enjoyable horror thriller in colour within the record time of three days! This would suggest, perhaps, that the medium for Corman is television, not films!

In 1964 Karloff filled a void in his repertoire when he appeared as a vampire in *Black Sabbath* (*I Tre Volti della Paura*) for American-International, a three-part 'demonthology' made in Italy with Karloff in the longest story, *The Wrudalak*, as the head vampire in an East European country, from a story by Leo Tolstoi. Wrudalaks are vampires that thirst for the blood of those they have loved most dearly. Karloff did his own English dubbing and the stories were linked by a commentary spoken by him. In the same year he also appeared in *Bikini Beach*, a Panavision and Technicolor American-International picture in which he had a guest appearance: seeing some teenagers fighting, he mutters to himself . . .'monsters'!

At Shepperton in 1965 he made *Monster of Terror* originally to be called *House at the End of the World* and entitled *Die, Monster, Die* in America; another Technicolor American-International film in which Karloff ends up as a hideous monster after starting the film as an ordinary, kindly man. The film was 'adapted', as the *Financial Times* put it, 'quite intelligently' from the original, and

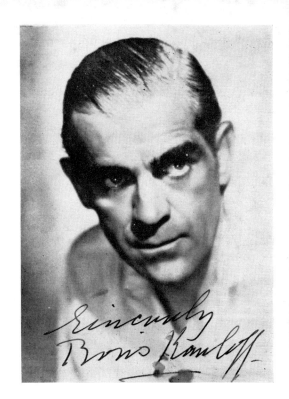

An autographed study that has been in the possession of the author for over twenty-five years.

Boris Karloff in 1907.

Karloff with Gloria Stuart in J B Priestley's *The Old Dark House* (Universal 1932, re-issued 1945).

A scene from *The Mask of Fu Manchu* (M-G-M 1932), based on the famous Sax Rohmer stories. The girl in oriental costume is Myrna Loy.

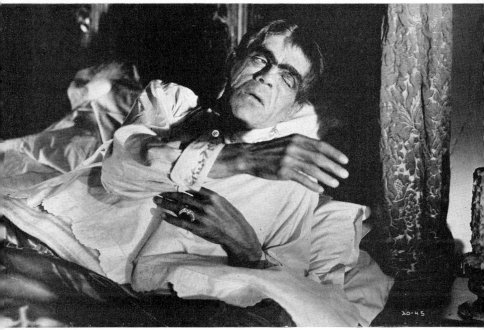

Boris Karloff in a scene from *The Ghoul*. Based on the novel by Frank King, this Gaumont-British film was released in 1933.

Gangster Karloff (centre) with George Raft (right) in what was perhaps the greatest of all gangster films: *Scarface*, directed by Howard Hawks for United Artists, 1932.

Boris Karloff in the Columbia production *The Black Room* directed by Roy William Neill, 1935.

The House of Rothschild, 1934. A 20th-Century Fox production, distributed by United Artists. Directed by Alfred Werker. In this scene Karloff is seen talking to George Arliss.

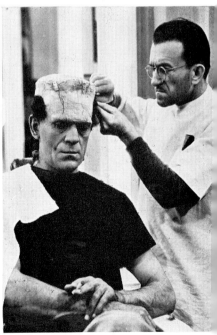

Universal's make-up wizard, Jack Pierce, working on Karloff for *The Bride of Frankenstein*.

Boris Karloff in his most famous screen role: the nameless monster in Mary Shelley's *Frankenstein* directed by James Whale. (Universal 1931, re-issued 1938.)

The Raven, a Universal thriller based on some of Edgar Allan Poe's tales of mystery and imagination. Directed by Louis Friedlander, 1935.

Boris Karloff as Fang, the Chinese bandit, in *West of Shanghai* (Warner Brothers, distributed by First National, 1937).

In *Juggernaut* (Twickenham Films) directed by Henry Edwards, 1936.

As he appeared in *The Walking Dead*, a Warner Brothers production, directed in 1936 by Michael Curtiz

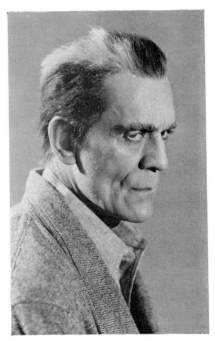

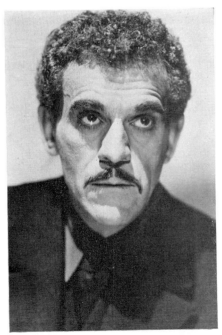

Karloff as the strange and remote being, brought back to life after electrocution: *The Walking Dead*, 1936.

Karloff in Universal's *The Invisible Ray*, 1936.

Boris Karloff as the supine monster in Universal's *Son of Frankenstein* with Bela Lugosi and Basil Rathbone, 1939.

Boris Karloff with Peter Lorre and band-leader Kay Kyser in the R K O Radio comedy-mystery-thriller *You'll Find Out*. Produced and directed by David Butler, 1941.

Isle of the Dead, 1945. An R K O Radio
film directed by Mark Robson.

Boris Karloff in *Bedlam*, 1946, with Glenn Vernon as The Gilded Boy in R K O
Radio's starkly realistic drama of 18th-century London. Not released in England.

Boris Karloff with Lucille Ball in the Hunt Stromberg production *Personal Column*, released through United Artists, directed by Douglas Sirk, 1947, re-issued 1955. Entitled *Lured* in U S A.

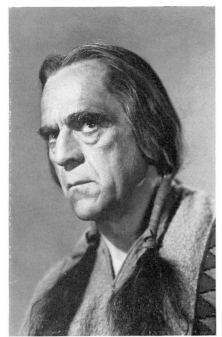

Boris Karloff as Tishomingo, the Choctaw Indian in the Universal-International film *Tap Roots* directed by George Marshall, 1948.

Boris Karloff as the one-eyed English detective in the 'death in the dressing room' sequence from *Colonel March Investigates* (Criterion Films, 1953).

The monster (Boris Karloff) leads London police a merry chase over the rooftops in Universal-International's *Abbott and Costello Meet Dr Jekyll and Mr Hyde*. Directed by Charles Lamont, 1953.

Young director Michael Reeves (left) talks to Tony Tenser and Boris Karloff on the set of *The Sorcerers* in February 1967. This Tony Tenser Films release was filmed in colour in London.

Boris Karloff in his favourite role –
cricketer!

Boris Karloff in 1967.

Mr and Mrs Boris Karloff at home in their London flat, 1963.

superb, story by H P Lovecraft, a master of horror fiction. It might be described as the first truly contemporary terror story set in the present and dealing with science-fiction threats from outer space, but also using classic Gothic terror ingredients. Karloff, a carpet-slippered and mumbling old man (Nahum Witley) pays frequent and mysterious visits to an underground room from which an unearthly light glows. He and his wife are visited by a young American scientist, Stephen Rheinhart (Nick Adams) who is engaged to the daughter of Witley and his wife Letitia (Freda Jackson) who is bedridden, and keeps her face covered with a heavy black veil because of a hideously disfiguring fungus. She pleads with Stephen to take her daughter Susan (Suzan Farmer) away from the old house, but her husband scoffs at the idea. Meanwhile Stephen makes enquiries about the family in the village and learns that Susan's grandfather died, but that the body was never seen afterwards. When he returns to the Witley house Stephen is attacked by a black-robed figure, but escapes. He is determined now to take Susan away and they are leaving when they notice a strange light gleaming from a mound of glittering crystals in the greenhouse and, driven back into the house by a storm, they discover Mrs Witley's room empty. As they search for her, the now crazy mother attacks them, then suddenly collapses and reveals her leprous appearance before crumbling into a black dust. Witley himself has changed into a monster fungus and lunges at his terrified daughter before falling over the bannister to crash on the floor below where his body shatters and disintegrates. The film was produced by Pat Green, one of the few successful women producers in the film industry; she had previously produced *The Tomb of Ligeia* and was production manager on *City Under the Sea* and *The Breaking Point* after ten years in the theatre, having her first job as unpaid assistant stage-manager at Richmond Theatre.

In 1966 Karloff appeared in colour again in *The Venetian Affair*, directed by Jerry Thorpe. The Venetian location photography was superb and Karloff, as a political scientist controlled by a drug, received acclaim for his characterisation and acting ability in the company of such young players as Robert Vaughan and Elke Sommer. 1967 saw *The Sorcerers*, which was shown at the Trieste Film Festival where Catherine Lacey obtained a 'Best Actors' award and Karloff was given a gold medal. Talking to Philip Jenkinson on British television in March 1968, Karloff spoke of his last British role as an expert in witchcraft in *The Curse of the Crimson Altar*, which he played from a bath chair. The film was made at a house at Harrow, reputed to be haunted after a suicide in the swimming-pool in the garden. Christopher Lee, also in *Curse of the Crimson Altar*, said he owed a 'very considerable debt of gratitude to Boris Karloff for his appearances as the Frankenstein monster really started the interest in horror films.' Tony Tenser produced *Curse of the Crimson Altar* and was co-producer of *The Sorcerers*. (Mrs Karloff tells me he has ideas for a Karloff Theatre in London.)

Karloff's last American film was *Targets* (made in 1968, but not released in Britain until the autumn of 1969) – 'remarkably good' as veteran film-critic Richard Mallett said in *Punch*. An unusual film with Karloff practically playing himself, a famous horror-movie actor who decides to retire from acting, and a virtually separate story about a clean-cut young American who goes gun-crazy and murders his wife and mother, and then, from a high vantage point, picks off drivers at will on a busy highway. When police begin to arrive he escapes and finds himself at a drive-in movie theatre where Karloff is making a farewell personal appearance at a showing of one of his films, *The Terror*. At the critical moment the sniper, who has been picking off members of the audience, finds himself between Karloff on the screen and Karloff in real life. His old magic still there, Karloff deals with the armed youngster with his walking stick. The film includes a fascinating clip from *The Criminal Code* and the result was a superb and appropriate swan-song for Karloff. It was the first film produced and directed by Peter Bogdanovich, who appeared in the film as Sam, the young director-writer who hoped Karloff would make a new film with him. Bogdanovich's direction shows the influence of the American directors he admires so much and seemed to combine the construction of Hitchcock, the wildness of Don Siegel's gangster movies and the baroque quality of Corman, with whom Bogdanovich has worked. A very personal film, this detached and chilling view of a world gone quietly mad, was most effective and produced one of the most (if not the most) moving performances Karloff ever gave.

The background, according to Hollis Alperton in the *Saturday Review*, is that Roger Corman 'had two days of work owed to him by Boris Karloff and he suggested to Bogdanovich that he make use of these two days, employ twenty minutes of *The Terror* and put together a feature.' Bogdanovich accepted the challenge and *Targets* was the result. Mrs Karloff told me that sets created for other films were used and the film was made in a great rush. Karloff himself was not particularly pleased with the result. 'Brilliantly directed,' said Ernest Betts in *The People*, 'this is a shocker different from anything you have seen.' The film was based on the mass murders committed by a psychopathic youth at Houston, Texas.

In 1968 Karloff wanted to go to Mexico City to make four films but his doctor forbade the project because of the effort the high altitude would have on his weakened lung; in the event he made the four films, which were to be his last, in five weeks on a co-production basis between Azteca Films and Columbia Pictures. These were *The Isle of the Snake People*, *The Fear Chamber*, *House of Evil* and *The Incredible Invasion*. By now he was very tired; the weather was hot and he had only half of one lung to breathe with so talking was difficult for him and every exertion an effort. He would be in a corner somewhere, seated in his wheelchair, an oxygen mask to his face, studying his lines and then when the director's call came it was as though the years fell away and Karloff would rise easily to his feet. In one of these last films there is a sequence in which he was required to bolt a door and he did this action and then suddenly a look of extreme pain crossed his face and he slumped against the wall. Almost everyone on the set took a step forward to help when Karloff looked round as the shooting stopped, the humour alight in his eyes; he had fooled everyone with his acting.

In over one hundred and sixty films Karloff portrayed practically every unpleasant character conceivable and just once, really, in 1937, he tried in a mild way, to rebel against playing horror roles but the critics and the public would have none of it. Some idea of how profitable the monster image was to Karloff can be judged by the fact that after his death it was reported that he left £165,000 in uncollected salary in Mexico. Horror, or rather terror as Karloff would have preferred it, brought him success, and, willy-nilly, he had to continue to shock and surprise audiences in picture after picture ever after.

To jointly celebrate Karloff's seventy-fifth birthday in 1962 and the fiftieth anniversary of Universal Studios, I had suggested to James Quinn, the British Film Institute director at that time, that the National Film Theatre put on a season of Karloff's films. They were keen on the idea, but had to abandon the project, when among other difficulties, they did not receive sufficient support from the various film companies concerned. However, they did put on a Special 'All-Night Horror Homage to Boris Karloff' on 1st November 1969, and I was pleased to contribute a short Introduction at the invitation of Ken Wlaschin, the Institute's Programme Director. The films shown, rather a motley bag, were *The Mummy* (1932); *House of Doom* (1934), entitled *The Black Cat* in America; Roger Corman's *The Raven* (1962); *Black Sabbath* (1964). In view of Karloff's well-known aversion to the word 'horror', I thought it was a pity the programme, instead of being called a 'Horror Homage' had not been billed as a 'Terror Tribute'! Still, Boris Karloff was past caring and it turned out to be a night to remember for students of horror films and for admirers of Karloff, the quiet actor who was a master of terror.

CHAPTER 10

Stage, Radio and Television

IN 1937 KARLOFF had appeared as a lovable, old inventor in the film *Night Key*; the following year he so scared America, in a radio adaptation of *The Evil Eye* on an Edgar Bergen–Charlie McCarthy show, that demands for an investigation were heard on the floor of the Senate! He continued broadcasting throughout most of 1938 when he took a vacation from films to play the lead in the successful NBC *Lights Out* dramas.

Samuel Grafton, who has told me how much he liked and admired Karloff, points out in his article in the American *Good Housekeeping*, that Karloff's reputation was such that although an extremely competent actor, schooled in hundreds of parts in his stock-company days, playwrights hesitated to put him in anything but terror roles, feeling that his name roused audience expectations of seeing ghouls in a graveyard at midnight!

Russel Crouse and Howard Lindsay solved this problem neatly in their production of *Arsenic and Old Lace*, which opened at the Fulton Theatre, New York, in January 1941, by having Karloff play Jonathan

Brewster, the homicidal brother of two daffy, old man-poisoning sisters, who is in a constant rage because people are always saying he looks like Boris Karloff. This Broadway play with Karloff ('a great success') in his most memorable stage role ran for over 1,400 performances, and lasted nearly four years. At first, Karloff was reluctant to 'do a play in New York' – an expression he hated – but which Russel Crouse had used when he went out to California to invite Karloff to take the part; and it was only after he had been assured that there was a part which everyone concerned thought he could do, that did not have to carry the play, that Karloff said he would be delighted and appeared throughout the run in New York and on tour – apart from one period when he had to leave to go and make a film that he owed a company. Samuel Grafton says that Crouse and Lindsay first sent Karloff a contract calling for a salary of $25 a week and 'throw money', ie, the privilege of keeping all coins tossed on to the stage by patrons! When they were made to pay him his regular stage rate of $2,000 a week, they accused him of being a grasping miser and at least once paid him his large weekly stipend with great sacks of nickels! Yet, when they tried to persuade him to invest in the production and as a wise, old strolling-player, Karloff refused, they held back $6,000 worth of stock for him, until the reviews were published. This extraordinary privilege produced for Karloff a profit of some $50,000. He loved playing in *Arsenic and Old Lace* because he needed almost no make-up: only two dabs of grease-paint to make his temples seem hollow. And the audience loved it too. Talking to me about this production of *Arsenic and Old*

Lace, Karloff described the play as 'magnificently written and beautifully played and directed.' As *Current Biography 1941 Who's Who and Why* (W H Wilson and Co, New York) puts it: 'When the shadow of a sinister newcomer falls on the living-room door in the peculiar household depicted in Joseph Kesselring's farcical murder mystery . . . there are squeals of delighted horror in the audiences . . . they know that they are about to behold in the flesh the screen's most celebrated menace . . .'

'The comedy parts in the play are what float me along,' said Karloff at the time. 'If it weren't for the delightful acting of Josephine Hull, Jean Adair and Allyn Joslyn, my part would go for nothing. I'm content to be the villain in every piece, because I know it is expected of me. I've played a few straight parts in pictures, but the audiences were sure I was going to do something terrible and I think they were sorry I didn't. That is what it means to be typed. Playing to an audience is great joy after years of acting before the camera. An audience's responses tell you everything, if you will listen. Sometimes they say, "Yes, that's funny, we'll laugh if you give us a chance." But if you hear coughing and rustling out in front, people are saying: "Don't do that. It's no use. We aren't noticing." The most beautiful thing of all is the complete stillness of an audience so intent that it scarcely breathes. I had almost forgotten these things. In pictures the director is your only audience.' Karloff began in *Arsenic and Old Lace* the trend towards what might be called 'terror-comedy', that subsequently blossomed in his many large and small screen appearances, and as long as he lived he regretted that other commitments prevented his playing the part in the Capra film or in the London stage production, in which he was invited to play.

In 1946, Karloff appeared at Hollywood and San Francisco as Gramps, the sympathetic grandfather, in *On Borrowed Time;* he loved playing the part and it was easily his favourite play. Then in 1948, J B Priestley, after initial doubts, agreed to him being cast as a college professor in the American production at The Music Box of Priestley's own favourite play: *The Linden Tree.* This part gave Karloff a chance to show his gentler acting abilities. It is the story of genial Professor Linden who, on his sixty-fifth birthday, finds pressure from his home and from his University, to retire gracefully and make way for younger men and new ideas. Some of his lines might almost have been Karloff himself speaking. Towards the end of the play, for example, he says, 'As long as there is work to do and I am able to do it, I want to do it.' and, earlier: 'I don't want to leave the crew and join the passengers.' This role of the wise, easy-going English professor utterly suited the whole personality of Boris Karloff, and his acting and characterisation in the New York stage production were widely acclaimed, drawing fine comment. J B Priestley himself told me how delighted he was with Karloff, but the play did not last. Mrs Karloff has said that Priestley never saw this particular production. 'Good God! Not Karloff!' he is reported to have said to producer Maurice Evans. 'Put his name on the placards and people will think *The Linden Tree* is about an axe murderer!'

In 1949, Karloff appeared at the Booth Theatre, New York, as Decius Heiss in *The Shop at Sly Corner* by Edward Percy, writer and dramatist (died 1968). With Reginald

Denham, Percy wrote the successful *Ladies in Retirement*. One critic wrote, 'Mr Karloff is too good a man to waste on such domestic banality'. And then at the end of September, 1949, the American *Newsreel* magazine explained: 'With practically no advance warning, Boris Karloff crept into millions of homes via radio and television' with his 'double-duty' affair: *Starring Boris Karloff*. It was, *Newsreel* reports, 'some of the creepiest entertainment yet broadcast and televised,' and Karloff enjoyed the busy weeks that followed, providing thrills and chills on the air. Although radio and video versions of *Starring Boris Karloff* used much the same script and cast, a quick day sufficed for his radio rehearsal, while video took up virtually the remaining six days of each week. The results were good radio shows and exceptionally good television programmes. On his initial show Karloff played a hangman, with Mildred Natwick as his horrified wife, and into this portrayal he put all his often unrecognised acting ability, coupled with enthusiasm for a challenging medium. Essentially a humble man, despite the fact that his fee from ABC also provided for the cast and story cost, he preferred to leave the selection of both to others. As always he was candidly reasonable when asked about playing 'non-Karloffian' roles: 'After all,' he would reply with a twinkling grin, 'I can't play Little Lord Fauntleroy, can I?'

In April 1950, he appeared as George Darling and as Captain Hook at the Imperial Theatre on Broadway in the record run of the Jean Arthur production of *Peter Pan* where he was able to combine his love of children and his ability to play terror roles. After the original *Frankenstein* monster, his role of the hook-armed Captain Hook is one of those he most enjoyed playing.

Writing in *Films and Filming* in November 1957, Karloff said: 'Children choose what they want to see in an entertainment. This was brought home to me during the run of Barrie's *Peter Pan*. Being interested in the children's reaction to the play, I invited a hoard of them to come along to the theatre. *Peter Pan*, as everybody knows, is a mixture of romanticism and adventure. The somewhat frightening exploits of Captain Hook are offset by the whimsy of Tinker Bell. The frightening element would possibly, one would think, stay in a child's mind far longer than the fairy element. After the final curtain I took them backstage and introduced them to the cast. Almost all the children would first want to meet Wendy and Tinker Bell and then they would want to put on the Captain's hook. Their first reaction when they looked at themselves in the mirror was to grunt and scowl and to make the same type of lurching gestures as does Frankenstein's monster.'

In 1950, too, Karloff found another outlet for his fondness for children. In New York he told, in his deep, rich voice with its slight lisp, bedtime stories over the air on a weekly disc show for children. Where only a few months previously his mail had consisted chiefly of requests for scaring the daylights out of people of all ages; now, a typical opening to his show would be: 'And now I will tell you the story of *The Owl and the Pussy Cat*', and he proceeded to do so in those soft, cultured tones, with British inflections. The whole thing started some months earlier when a New York producer asked Karloff how he would like to be a disc-jockey. 'What on earth do you mean?' asked Karloff, who had played many parts but had never been a disc-jockey. 'For children, entirely for children,' explained the producer. And the deal was on.

For half an hour, from one of New York's largest radio stations, Karloff told stories, posed quizzes and spun records, which he chose himself. 'I never talk down to children,' he said at the time, 'I just put things over to them in simple language. I read from the classics, play really good recordings and then, perhaps, throw in some sneaky sound effects such as creaky hinges or a ship's bell tolling. But I always end my programme with some gay and happy music and good is always victorious over evil.'

In 1951, when he left Hollywood and turned largely to television, he took a luxurious apartment in New York. On television the 'gag value' of his reputation for inspiring terror was exploited in frequent guest appearances, at some thousands of dollars per half-hour. His appearance in a Donald O'Connor show was typical of the work he was doing at this period . . . Donald, as an aspiring young playwright, has an appointment to call on Karloff. He goes to Karloff's house, quivering with fright, and finds Karloff in a smock, peacefully working at sculpture. Donald speaks loudly and Karloff jumps. 'You frightened the life out of me!' Karloff protests and the audience roared. Playing against his reputation, Karloff then did a song and dance with O'Connor; his voice, low, deep and musical, was considered one of the most extraordinary in show business. He had a gift for comedy and loved these television appearances in which he hid his more sombre talents, because they allowed him to play something besides a monster.

During 1953 (Coronation Year), it was proposed by Cyril Enfield and Peter Daubeny to team Karloff with Hermione Gingold in a revue in England; alas, nothing came of the idea. Mrs Evelyn Karloff has told me that her husband would have loved to have acted on the London stage but he was too old to do so when the opportunity occurred.

From New York Karloff began to make frequent trips to England and on one of these visits he recorded a play that was broadcast on British radio some months later in December 1953. Karloff appeared as Sir Francis Brittain in *Hanging Judge*. Produced by Cleland Finn, in *The Play of his Choice* series, *Hanging Judge* was written by well-known actor Raymond Massey who adapted it from a novel by Bruce Hamilton. The action takes place between the two World Wars. The play has a controversial interest in that it discusses the possibility of an innocent man being hanged for murder. There seems no doubt in the case of the prisoner when Mr Justice Brittain sentences him to death in the opening moments of the play, but the judge is not convinced; yet he holds unyieldingly to the view that the British Judicial system, at least where it covers a capital charge, is infallible and it is only later in the play when it is revealed that the Judge, played by Boris Karloff, has been leading a 'double life' of some depravity for over thirty years that the real core of the play becomes apparent.

Karloff broke right away from terror roles in 1954 to play a Scotland Yard detective with a patch over one eye in a series of twenty-six television films under the title *Colonel March of Scotland Yard*. These highly-successful half-hour films were shown on British television for over three years, although they had originally been made for the United States market. Karloff played the genial, but shrewd, police investigator from the Department of Queer Complaints, the series being based on John Dickson Carr's book of that title. Bringing a sombre dignity to the films, which were frequently repeated, Karloff's wonderful speaking voice came as a welcome change from the harsh and sometimes inarticulate 'twang' of many popular actors. His natural humour and kindly approach was allowed to come over in these films to a greater extent than it had ever done in the past, and watching them one could not help realising how far Karloff had come since his early film days; yet the admiration for the mature acting and presentation was inevitably tinged with nostalgia when one recalled his title roles in films like *The Ghoul; The Mummy* and, of course, his Frankenstein's monster.

In England again, in 1955, he appeared on the stage of the London Palladium in *Night of a 100 Stars*, an annual charity-show organised to raise funds for the Actors' Orphanage. As Peter Noble, writer, film-critic and actor himself, told me, it was a great night. Peter Noble, who had been appearing weekly in the currently popular BBC television panel show, *Find the Link*, took part, together with Laurence Olivier, Danny Kaye, John Mills, Marlene Dietrich, Alec Guiness, Diana Dors, Eric Portman, the Crazy Gang, Gilbert Harding, Jack Hawkins, Beatrice Lillie, Hermione Baddeley, Michael Redgrave, Bernard Braden, Pat

Kirkwood, Emlyn Williams and Richard Attenborough together with many other stars – and Boris Karloff was teamed in a sketch with, of all people, Hermione Gingold of the mordant humour, undoubtedly the 'wicked aunt' of English show business, until she took out American naturalisation papers in 1959. But there can only ever be one Miss Gingold or 'Mother Gingold' as she prefers to be known. It was, of course, Hermione Gingold, as Charles Graves relates in his story of the Café de Paris: *Champagne and Chandeliers* (London, 1958) who made her entrance for cabaret at the Café de Paris by sliding down the famous stairs, murmuring, 'Hush, hush, whisper who dares, old Mother Gingold is coming down stairs.'

Back in New York, Karloff played Bishop Cauchon in Jean Anouilh's *The Lark*, which opened in November 1955, and ran into the following year at the Longacre Theatre. Julie Harris played the title role of Joan of Arc and both she and prosecutor Karloff repeated their roles on television the following year. Indeed, he did a great deal of television and radio work in America at this time.

A few months after *The Lark* finished, Karloff did not have to ask what role he would be playing when he was asked to take part in the American television version of *Little Red Riding Hood* on Rosemary Clooney's weekly show! He was fitted out with a long, bushy tail and given a full-length nightgown. And when Miss Clooney came upon him languishing woefully in her grandmother's bed, his response to her enquiry was a croaking chorus of 'You'd be surprised'! 'It's a part I'd never played before,' Karloff told me, but he put in a fine performance and the only difficulty he encountered was that his tail got in his way when he sat down!

Still playing 'against the character', recording impresarios had Karloff make a series of children's records which with his incredible voice he did magnificently – and his rendering of *Happy Times Records* with *Tales of Mystery and Imagination*, *The Legend of Sleepy Hollow* and *Rip Van Winkle* are little masterpieces. An authority on fairy tales, he once picked up over £5,000 answering questions about them on a New York quiz show. Karloff's participation in recording *Tales from Hans Andersen* for Caedmon Literary Series was particularly successful. There was *Mother Goose*, directed by Howard O Sackler with music by Hershy Kay, the distinguished American composer who endowed the lovely traditional melodies and nursery-rhymes with imaginative, modern arrangements; and its rollicking songs included Boris Karloff singing a lusty *Old King Cole* and the recitation in his most 'monstrous' manner of 'There was a Crooked Man . . .' made the recording a memorable experience of the happiest kind – a children's record that was relished by adults. For Caedmon, he also recorded Kipling's *The Jungle Book* and some Shakespeare.

Karloff was one of the first actors to take up television and it proved very profitable for him. In Hollywood he hosted sixty-six programmes of the weekly *Thriller* series and acted in five of them: *The Prediction*, *The Premature Burial*, *The Last of the Sommervilles* (adapted and directed by Ida Lupino), *Dialogues with Death* and *The Incredible Doktor Markesan*. These continued to be shown for the next ten years on independent stations throughout the United States and in 1967 some of them appeared on Westward Television in England. At the home of William Fyne, producer of the *Thriller* series, Karloff remarked that thirty years after playing the monster for Universal, he was back on the same lot, as host for *Thriller* and 'in a way, its almost like coming home again.' Critics and public agreed that he was especially good in a *Suspicion* programme on 9th December 1957, called *The Deadly Game* and in the adaptation of Washington Irving's immortal story *The Legend of Sleepy Hollow* in the *Shirley Temple Storybook* programme on 7th March 1958, where he appeared as Father Knickerbocker; and as Billy Bones in *Treasure Island* in the Du Pont programme.

Meanwhile, in 1957 he appeared on British television in Alan Melville's *A to Z* programme; Karloff's contribution being the letter 'X' for horror films. The shows were produced by Brian Sears and Alan Melville told me that Boris Karloff did the filming 'in a tearing hurry to get back to California' as he was filming; but it was a very real pleasure for English audiences to see him 'in the flesh' on television. Later, he appeared on British radio in Jack de Manio's *Today* series, as I learned when I appeared on the same programme some years later. I had previously met de Manio at one of the Authors of the Year Parties at the lofty Martini Terrace of New Zealand House following publication of his delightful book of reminiscences of the BBC, *Life with Auntie*, and he told me how much he had enjoyed talking to Boris Karloff. Karloff was also seen on British television as a guest celebrity on *What's my Line?*, a quiz programme.

Actually 1957 was an important year for horror addicts, especially in America where a number of old Universal classics were released in a package deal and were seen on television under the general title *Shock Theatre*. They were shown three nights a week, on

Thursdays, Fridays and Saturdays, and achieved a high audience rating. At the same time, Hammer Films in England made a new Frankenstein film, *The Curse of Frankenstein*, which grossed an enormous profit and helped to establish the studio as one of the great producers of horror films. Also in production at this time, for release the following year, was Hammer's new version of *Dracula*, in colour, starring Christopher Lee in the title role and with Peter Cushing as his persistent adversary, Dr Van Helsing.

On Whit Monday 1960, Karloff appeared in the nineteenth century cricketing melodrama presented by The Company of Lord's Taverners: *Upgreen – and at 'em or A Maiden Nearly Over*, on British television, produced by Ronald Marsh. All the members of the cast, including Jimmy Edwards, Jack Warner, Brian Rix and Richard Attenborough, were members of the Lord's Taverners and all the artists gave their fees to the National Playing Fields Association, which benefited by something like £2,500, the Taverners having already raised over £60,000 for this charity. Karloff opened the play arrayed in nightshirt and nightcap as 'the Faithful Butler'. The Lord's Taverners are a brotherhood of cricket lovers who derive their name from one of the world's most congenial hostelries, the Tavern at Lord's Cricket Ground.

In June 1962 Karloff was guest star in *The Dickie Henderson Show* on British Independent television. It was always the terror gag that provided the spice for these enterprises, either directly because he was being frightening, or indirectly because it was so amusing that he wasn't being frightening. In America there was the

annual animated Christmas favourite from the pen of
contemporary Theodor Seuss Geisel, 'Dr Seuss': *How
the Grinch Stole Christmas* (shown on British television –
1967) and various dramatic performances.

During the summer of the same year he introduced the
British ABC Television science-fiction series *Out of This
World*. As Karloff said in an article published in *TV Times*,
22nd June 1962, 'Science-fiction is not only strange,
it combines the aspects of terror and excitement with
stories that set the spine tingling. Many other stories have
all these qualities. But with science-fiction there is the
added dimension – the fact that this could happen.' The
series, and Karloff introduced and closed each story, was
composed of varied and imaginative, but not too far-
fetched stories that were very effective, not least because
of the heightening atmosphere provided by the presence
of Boris Karloff. Also in 1962, Karloff finally agreed to
don his Frankenstein make-up again, after thirty-
one years, for the Canadian Broadcasting Company's
production, *Route 66*. And in the years that followed
he was frequently seen on television in America and
Britain.

In 1968 he revelled in the role of the dotty THRUSH
menace, Mother Muffin, as he stalked Napoleon Solo
and April Dancer through an episode of *The Girl from
UNCLE*. In one of his last appearances, broadcast in
Britain on 12th July 1969, he played the sympathetic
role of Mikhail Orlo from a bath chair in *The White
Birch* in *The Name of the Game* series, this one concerning
the invasion of Czechoslovakia by Russian troops.
Karloff played the role of the author of a book con-
fiscated by the Russians. He wanted the book smuggled

out of the country so that the royalties could go to the Czech freedom fighters.

During 1968/9 the Colonel March series and the *I Spy* series were shown on Portuguese television; while some idea of the enormous amount of television work Karloff did in America is evident from the fact that he took part in over eighty shows from 1949 when he appeared in *Five Golden Guineas* to 1968 when he was featured in the Jonathan Winters Show. Between these dates he portrayed such varied characters as Rasputin in a *Suspense* play and King Arthur in a NBC *Spectacular*; he appeared in the *Robert Montgomery Theatre*, the *Frankie Lane Show*, the *Red Skelton Show*, the *$64,000 Question*, the *Hallmark Hall of Fame*, the *Kate Smith Show*, the *Gale Storm Show*, the *Dinah Shore Show*, the *Betty White Show* and the *Gary Moore Show*. He appeared in episodes of the *Columbia Workshop*, the *Lux Theatre*, *Climax, Down You Go, Elgin Hour, Who Said That?, I've Got a Secret, U.S. Steel Show, Aloca Hour, Lux Video Theatre, Suspicion, Telephone Time, Studio One, Plymouth Playhouse, Playhouse 90, World Stage, Reckoning, Du Pont Show of the Month, Hollywood Sings, Out of This World, Theatre 62, Chronicle, Wild Wild West, I Spy, The Girl from UNCLE* and of course the excellent *Thriller* series. During that last performance on television in the Jonathan Winters Show at Hallowe'en he was walking heavily with a stick and was practically confined to a wheelchair with oxygen always close at hand, yet he astounded everyone by almost bounding on to the stage, apparently full of stamina, and he stole the show with a straightforward talking version of *It was a Very Good Year*. In addition he appeared in half-a-dozen television commercials, advertising May Butternut Coffee, Schaeffer Pens, Volkswagen cars, Ronson products and A1 sauce. In Britain he was seen in an advertisement for beer.

It was in 1959 that Boris Karloff had returned to England for good. 'I'm home at last', he said as he stepped with his wife from a transatlantic Comet at London Airport.

CHAPTER 11

Boris Karloff — the Complete Man

IT MUST HAVE been a poignant moment for Boris Karloff when he returned home to England on 1st May 1959; fifty years almost to the day from when he had first left these shores to seek his fortune in the New World on 7th May 1909. 'I've been away too long,' said the bespectacled but keen-eyed actor, looking wonderfully bronzed and fit and sporting a clipped moustache. He looked, in fact, exactly what he was: a silver-haired and cultivated English gentleman, with the slightly bow legs which only the most reliable sort of English clubman was ever known to possess. 'Yes, I'm home at last. I have been back many times over the past few years but never before have I been able to say that with feeling.' Did he ever think of applying for American citizenship? 'No, sir. I owe my success and my money to America; but I would be a hypocrite if I became anything but British.' What made him finally sever his American residential connexions? 'I think that every Englishman wants to,' he replied simply and I recalled that he had told me that on the first night of his first visit to England in twenty-four years, in 1933, he hadn't slept a wink, sitting in his hotel bedroom at an open window until dawn, filling his eyes with the sight of London and his lungs with the odour of it. Next day he started work filming and for the next six weeks he was kept too busy to dwell nostalgically on the magic of England, but afterwards he did spend three weeks doing what he had dreamed of doing; visiting Uppingham and eating a meal in the big dining-room there – and finding the plum pudding just as good as he had always remembered it! He bought buns in the 'Tuck Shop' and he wandered and dawdled in the fresh green countryside, stopping at little inns and enjoying a leisurely cup of English tea each day at four in the afternoon. 'It is a part of English life to take time to enjoy the quiet things,' he used to say.

Mrs Dorothy Karloff wrote of this visit to England in an American magazine in which she tells of house-hunting in Surrey and Sussex with 'Boris's brother Sir John Pratt and Lady Pratt' and of the atmosphere and hospitality at 'a real English inn.' While Karloff was at the studio his wife tells of lunching with Joyce Grenfell and Lady Mary Campbell and of supper with 'Boris at the Savoy Grill where you see everyone in the theatrical world at some time or another, they say . . . that night Noel Coward, Robert Kane, Michael Balcon, Florence Desmond and Gertrude Lawrence were there *and* the Karloffs. We had a grand time and walked home through a late Spring snowfall. Imagine in May!' Eventually they found their house: The Old Malt House, Hurley, and here Mrs Dorothy Karloff tried hard to interest her husband in parties and socializing. There were bridge parties 'with Lady Montague'; dinners with 'royalty, no less: Princess Toubitsky and Prince and Princess Lowenstein' followed, at Karloff's suggestion I am sure, by a visit to the local pub, *The Chequers* where they stayed for hours, 'eating cheese and watercress and drinking ale.' They 'didn't get home until the wee hours, so I claim it to be a perfect night's entertainment' says Mrs Karloff. One wonders what Boris thought!

Boris and Evie Karloff had bought a top floor flat in a large, Victorian house in Cadogan Square when they were here in 1958; their furniture was shipped over from the United States and they moved in without delay.

Miss Adrienne Corri, who had worked with Karloff in England on *Corridors of Blood*, had foretold that this 'gentlest monster' was going to finally settle in England, during a television interview with Peter Haigh in *Picture Parade* in August 1958. Miss Corri said that Karloff was the most popular man on the set while making *Corridors of Blood* and he was the first actor she had ever heard of for whom all the technicians clubbed together to buy him a farewell present on the completion of the film.

In working on this biography I have come across numerous examples of the respect and affection with which Karloff was regarded by everyone with whom he came in contact. As Archie Nathan put it in his fascinating *Costumes by Nathan* (Newnes, 1960), 'amongst the very interesting films we have recently dressed are what is known as 'horror' films – and how very different from the ghastly characters he portrays is that gentle person Boris Karloff.' Whether the occasion was the opening of a new public house in London for a friend; acting Santa Claus for crippled children at a hospital in

America or simply helping and encouraging, as he invariably did, the new and young actors and technicians in films and television – Karloff continued his life-long habit of doing good turns for everyone whenever he could. A monster he may have been in film fiction, but in fact Karloff was a typical and charming English gentleman of the old school. During the making of one of his last films Mrs Terri Pinckard, a well-known Hollywood hostess, was present with her nine-year-old son. Karloff was posing for some photographs and during a rest he called the boy to him. 'Oh Mr Karloff,' gasped the awestruck child, 'I've waited and waited for this moment!' The lookers-on laughed but Karloff took the matter seriously as he always did with children and pulling the boy towards him, he turned to the photographer and said: 'The next few will be of the boy and I together.' A great lover of children, a gigantic cricket enthusiast, a keen gardener and lover of flowers, he grew in stature with the years as his hair turned white and the sinister and dark tones in his skin lightened. Yet his name was so firmly linked with horror in the public mind that audiences going to a theatre or cinema to see Karloff were half-scared to begin with! Every filmgoer's memories include Karloff limping, leering and lurching through dozens of films; some good, some bad and some mediocre.

A great reader (his London flat possesses several hundred books: works on the theatre, cricket, antiques, painting and music) and a thoroughly literate man, American publishers had him edit two anthologies: a collection of ghost stories called *Tales of Terror* for Tower Books in 1943, and reprinted the same year; and a collection of poems and stories of horror and the supernatural entitled *And the Darkness Falls* for the World Publishing Company in 1946. He selected all the material for both books himself, the second one while he was touring in *Arsenic and Old Lace*. He also contributed an introduction to Charles Addams' *Drawn and Quartered*, and in 1965 *The Boris Karloff Horror Anthology* was published simultaneously by Souvenir Press in London and Ryerson Press in Canada. In the short introduction, Karloff endeared himself to connoisseurs of stories of this *genre* when he said: 'There is something very satisfying about a good horror story.'

Still in the world of books he must have felt at home in June 1954 when he opened the Crime Writers' Association's first exhibition in Albermarle Street, holding a skeleton's hand as he spoke! 'I see a friendly and familiar face here,' he said, with a sideways glance at the skeleton. 'I hope it will be in order if I hold his hand while I speak; it may give me Dutch courage!' Karloff, who had flown from America for the exhibition, thanked the crime writers for the material they had given him. 'Thank you, too, for the many happy hours I can have sitting at Lord's – under a tarpaulin – reading crime books!'

When he was twenty-two Karloff nearly won a fortune. In later years he used to say that he was glad he hadn't and he looked upon the fact as a stroke of good luck. Here perhaps for a moment we can glimpse the real Boris Karloff and his philosophy: the man behind the mask. But let him tell the story in his own words:

'Probably one of the greatest things that happened to me was in Vancouver when I was twenty-two years old.

Someone offered me a half interest in a goldmine for £100. I had the money too. I asked the advice of a banker friend and he said, "No." That mine was subsequently sold for £3,000,000. But imagine what would have happened to me. It would have ruined me.'

Looking back over those early years of struggle, a reminiscent smile would hover over Karloff's face; but it was always other people he thought of first and then the 'luck' that he always talked about: 'All you can do in life,' he said in 1968, 'is get some experience, stick at it, and hope you will be lucky. Luck is all important. Being in the right place at the right time makes all the difference.'

'I shall never forget those early days of struggle and the great kindness of some of my landladies who let my rent go for months at a time. The accidents of chance have, without a doubt, played their part in my life. I realise that the luck element means so much to a man. In my own case, there were at least a hundred men with better character experience, who knew their acting business thoroughly, who might have had the same opportunity that I did. I got the break. They didn't. That's the story. You could heave a brick out of the window and hit ten actors who could play my parts. But I happened to be on the right corner at the right time when the chance came along. But for a chapter of accidents, I'd be in the same position I was long before *Frankenstein*. I know many character men, some of whom I played with in 1920. They were getting much more money than I was then, but in the latter 1930s they found the going extremely hard. Some of them did an occasional day's work as extras. That is about the end of one's hopes of getting anywhere in Hollywood. I drove a lorry for a year and a half to avoid taking the leap of signing up at the Central Casting Bureau. In many ways I'm very glad I did not get the break when I was younger. I might not have had the sense to hold on to my good fortune. Luckily, it came to me in the prime of my life, when I'd sufficient experience to know what to do. I'll never forget those early days and I'm very grateful for the many people who helped and encouraged me. Places, too, have a big pull on your heart strings and some day I'd like to journey again through the little towns of Canada and the north-western part of the United States, where I played with repertory companies . . . although, you know, there is a sadness about returning to remembered places, a sadness that often overshadows joy – but it is a sweet sorrow, if taken in small doses.' . . . 'Many parts of the American continent are beautiful.' he told me, 'but there is nothing in the world to match the beauty of the English countryside.'

On growing old, he once said: 'Fun is fun, but you don't want to get to a point where you become a nuisance to yourself and everyone else. Our vices are our virtues run to seed, aren't they? That can be true of living too long.' On his death in February 1969, his wife remarked on the fact that he had died, as he would have wished to die, in harness.

He always called his success 'just a lucky break'. 'The odd thing is,' he told me once, 'that however bad things were I never lost faith in my luck; that's why, when I was on the rocks with only four or five dollars in the world, I would always spend it. Twice I have been down to five cents. I somehow knew I shouldn't starve, that I should come through; that something would happen – and it always did.' And the friends of those not-so-prosperous days were always very much his friends. He once made a special trip across America to see an old friend of his early stock days who was ill, and to ensure that he was being properly cared for. Karloff always insisted on giving everyone but himself credit for his amazing rise to stardom. 'I've been lucky,' he used to say, 'I've had an incredible life, a darn good life . . .'

But it takes more than luck to reach the heights of acting ability and the regard and affection with which Boris Karloff was acclaimed on both sides of the Atlantic. As the late John Paddy Carstairs points out in his *Hadn't We the Gaiety?*, 'only a genius could have thought of the name Boris Karloff and known that the chances of being a success in filmland are ten times more possible with just a name.' And how true that is: Boris Karloff – the very name is a shudder.

Karloff said once: 'a shoemaker should stick to his last and a monster should stick to his monstrosities. At least, that's been my story and I'm going to stick to it! Of course, I know this is not the popular point of view. Most of the chaps who occasionally act in the weird nightmare sort of roles that have been my constant screen fare, do so rather unwillingly. They would much prefer playing something a trifle more romantic. But I really enjoy portrayals of grotesque characters; they fascinate me, and they have brought me stardom and a handsome income. I protest though against the labelling of my melodramas as horror pictures. They are bogy stories, that's all. Just bogy stories with the same appeal as thrilling ghost stories or fantastic fairy tales that entertain and enthrall in spite of being so much hokum.'

It used to be his great fear (it is the fear of all actors who play terror roles) that someday he might be trying to scare people and they'd laugh instead. 'You play it very close to the edge of comedy,' Karloff reminisced.

And yet this man who was mild of manner, benign, and with a perfect English public school accent was not afraid to be outspoken on occasions. 'Censorship of any sort is a fearful thing.' he told Herbert Kretzmer of the *Daily Sketch* in 1958, 'and the word DON'T is the most terrifying in the language.'

'I am opposed to censorship in any form,' he said in his 1957 article in *Films and Filming*. 'Censorship always seems to me to be a mistrust of people's intelligence. I believe that good taste takes care of licence. It is also worth remembering that one does not have to go and see a film. Naturally, good taste plays a very important part in the telling of a horror story on film. Some have taste, others regrettably have not. As there are no rules laid down to give an indication of good taste it is up to the film's makers. You are walking a very narrow tight-rope when you make such a film. It is building the illusion of the impossible and giving it the semblance of reality that is of prime importance. The moment the film becomes stupid the audience will laugh and the illusion is lost . . . never to be regained. The story must be intelligent and coherent as well as being unusual and bizarre . . . in fact just like a fairy tale or a good folk story. The 'horror' has to be for the sake of the story and not, as a few films have done, have a story outline just for the sake of injecting as many shocks as possible.

'The central character is most important in a horror picture because he is more complex. You must understand his point of view although you know he is mistaken. You must have sympathy for him although you know he is terribly wrong. Although you are pleased to see him destroyed you are sorry that it has happened. The special technique of horror film-acting is to stimulate the imagination. This is usually done by showing bits and pieces which gradually build up a picture in people's imagination.'

In the middle 'thirties a few critics were suggesting that Karloff's acting left much to be desired. It was implied that the distorted features that marked so many of his films were so hynotic that it was difficult to decide whether or not Karloff could actually act, or was merely a stereotyped 'ugly'. It was said that he held his own and often gave a good account of himself from his earliest films as he did right through most of the 'forties, but later there is some justification for comments that he occasionally 'walked through' a role which he did not respect and one thinks in particular of *Voodoo Island* and *Frankenstein 1970*: neither film had much cinematic quality or opportunity for expressing acting ability. In fact Karloff's varied interpretations and intelligent delivery enabled him to rise above mere character acting. The charge that he gave slovenly performances on occasions does not bear scrutiny. If the script of half-a-dozen pictures called for a kindly scientist to test some remarkable discovery in an illegal manner, for which he became enraged at being punished; it may be an actor's duty to play the role in the same way and yet when this happened to Karloff in such

films as *The Man They Could Not Hang, Before I Hang,
The Ape, Behind the Door* and *The Devil Commands*, he
played each character individually and with warmth
and expression and it is no exaggeration to say that
Karloff never disgraced himself or his profession by
playing roles that the public demanded of him.

A man of remarkable personal energy, compassion
and intelligence, he worked long and hard in America
to improve the lot of the film actor in the early days,
and the Screen Actors Guild was one of the big things
in his life. Mrs Karloff told me that he was one of the
twelve founders of the Guild in 1932 who drew for the
first dozen membership cards and Karloff drew No. 9.
Later he had a Gold Life Membership Card which was
always one of his most treasured possessions. Always very
keen on improving the status of the actor, the SAG was
formed without the cooperation of much of the film
production industry, and I heard about the early meet-
ings held behind locked doors when producers and
directors and executives were not around, and of the
years that Karloff served on the administrative side of
the Guild. Ten days after his gold award for *The Sorcerers*,
when the film was shown at the Trieste Film Festival,
the Karloff's Kensington flat was burgled, Mrs Evelyn
Karloff told me. This medal was taken and lots of other
valuables including wedding presents and a unique gold
charm bracelet which the Karloff's really treasured: it
carried many mementos of their life together and included
a tiny gold book with Karloff's films engraved on it.
They took, too, Mrs Karloff's gold watch and she has
now taken to wearing her husband's wrist watch.
Nothing was ever recovered.

Cricket always remained his great love. Stepping off the liner at Plymouth in 1952 on one of his visits to England, his first words to reporters were: 'Let's forget *Frankenstein;* this is just the weather for cricket.' On that occasion, too, he said: 'I've given up playing now – but I'm looking forward to Lord's and Dennis Compton. Old Aubrey Smith really got the game going in Hollywood. Basil Rathbone played sometimes; so did Clive Brook. Now there are six teams there but the game will never take on in America. It's quite foreign to their temperament. British cricket is in a perilous position financially. The grounds are half-empty. Sunday cricket would make the world of difference to the gates. I'm all for it. British cricket is magnificent . . .'

Now that he is gone, memories crowd in of this essentially English man; kindly, soft-spoken, and sporting his old school tie; fond of gardening and positively punch-drunk about cricket; his face deeply tanned, mirroring nothing of the sinister parts he played so often on stage and screen. For a few years he and his wife lived quietly in their Knightsbridge flat furnished with the impeccable good taste that was reflected in everything about him, even down to his grey embossed notepaper with the neat *BK* in red on the back of the envelope. He flew to America from time to time for film making and television work, and once a week he recorded at his home a digest of *Readers Digest* for American radio. He did this particular radio work all over the world and the programmes were broadcast from some four hundred American radio stations for twelve years. The Karloffs collected unusual furniture and antiques and before long the flat was too small for them. They found a larger flat in Kensington and a delightful cottage in the depths of Hampshire, and there Boris Karloff happily spent his last years.

Recognising the handsome features and the singular gait, people catching a glimpse of Karloff on London streets or near the lovely and unusual cottage not far from the sea, would turn to their companions and use the most famous misquotation in English literature: 'There goes Frankenstein', for Baron Frankenstein was, of course, the scientist who created the monster which, in the film as in the book, had no name. It was a simple mistake, but one that was not easily put right and indeed it will probably never now be universally corrected; but Boris Karloff didn't mind, he went unhurriedly on his way with his self-expressed intention to 'carry on and live as well and as fully' as he could. 'It's a curious thing,' he said to me once, 'but I sort of tasted blood as the Demon King in my first stage part sixty years ago, and I knew right then and there that that was what I wanted to do for the rest of my life. And if you want something that badly, there's only one thing to do – go out and get it. It's the only way: it's a tough life, it's a rough life and only a handful of people are successful – they're the lucky ones, and it is luck. You've learned the A B C of your craft, your business or your profession; then who is going to be lucky? Who's going to be on the right corner at the right moment? And nine people out of ten must resign themselves to lives of deprivation and some-times frustration and the handful who are lucky, are very lucky and should be very grateful. And the only thing that makes it worthwhile with the odds so heavily loaded against you is if it is the only thing you really love doing and the only thing you really want to do.

If you don't go into it with what Conrad called the "obscure inner urge", it's no good; for God's sake don't but if you have it then for God's sake do!'

In the summer of 1963, at seventy-six years of age, he signed a four-year contract for still more 'monster' films, and in February, 1964, he began work on *House at the End of the World* (later *Monster of Terror*) at Shepperton Studios, where he played true to form and ended up a mass of fungus! At Shepperton the seventy-seven year-old, white-haired actor talked about his acting life. He was adamant that he would retire only in death. 'Ever since I first came really alive with my first taste of being an actor', he said in his quiet, cultured voice, 'I have always "died" a little when not working. I am never really alive unless I am at work, merely recharging for the next spell. To know that I was never to act again would be something akin to a death sentence for me.' 'Yesterday is always supposed to have been better than today,' he told me 'I don't believe it; the present and the future is always better than the past.'

In a special feature, *My Life of Terror*, distributed while he was making *Monster of Terror*, everyone was told for the first time that an arthritic knee, which had troubled him for years, had finally begun to dictate a less active world, but 'it hasn't dimmed his relish for good food, good company and lots of good talk. He is not typical of his age in that he does not necessarily dismiss contemporary life as a deterioration of what has past. But he insists that young people must, in turn, recognise that there were some pretty good things when he was young. He is not much of a television fan but he cites the very moving television tribute to Sir Winston

Churchill as a clue to the question: why has he always remained absolutely British?'

'I have a great regard for the American people', he said, 'but watching that very moving funeral, I experienced that intangible something that tells a person that he 'belongs'. If I, myself, never quite knew for certain why I never became an American citizen before that cold Saturday morning, I was left in no doubt later. Here I belong. Here is my ultimate home. And it goes a damn sight deeper than I can say.' 'I have only one regret about coming home,' he once said to me, 'the regret is that I didn't do it sooner!'

In April 1966 Karloff gave what he described as his 'first major press reception in forty years.' It took place at Milt Larsen's fantastic Magic Castle, an old mansion where magicians meet, off Franklin Avenue up the hill behind the famous Grauman's Chinese Theatre. The occasion was to celebrate the Decca Record Album (DL 4833), *An Evening with Boris Karloff and his Friends* which features scenes from *Bride of Frankenstein* and *Son of Frankenstein*. The recording was released in Britain under the Brunswick label (LAT 8678). The script, by Forrest Ackerman, is a more or less straightforward documentary of Karloff's life and times with the recorded voices of Bela Lugosi, Lionel Atwill, Colin Clive, Ernest Thesiger, Elsa Lanchester, Edward van Sloan and Dwight Frye. The script, read by Karloff, was all taped with very few fluffs or retakes, in less than an hour. Asked to what he attributed his remarkable vitality, Karloff would always reply: 'Oh! I don't know. Just good clean living, I suppose – up to the age of six!' The Magic Castle had been elaborately decorated for the occasion with rare posters, lobby portraits and enlarged stills. It is in the forecourt of Grauman's Chinese Theatre that the handprints, footprints and signatures of screen 'immortals' are preserved and in 1967 there was talk of Karloff being asked to add his marks to those of such film personalities as Mary Pickford, Clark Gable and Al Jolson, but nothing came of the suggestion. A couple of years before his death there was a campaign to get Karloff some kind of special Oscar at the Academy Awards, recognizing his unique contribution to motion pictures; unhappily this was not successful. He did receive two *Ann Radcliffe Awards* for outstanding contributions to the Gothic field in films and a *Count Dracula Award* was scheduled for presentation to him during that society's seventh annual dinner which took place after his death, and an empty chair was reserved in his honour.

Boris Karloff was never allowed to forget that as Frankenstein's monster he became famous overnight for having the most frightening face in the world. This scion of a distinguished family retained to the end of his life an odd fondness for that monster, but in later days he was also known as a comedian, a fine actor, and one of the gentlest gentlemen in show business. People who met him a dozen times and more were never really sure that he recognized them for he was always so very careful to ensure that he would cause no embarrassment to anyone and so he really seemed to prefer not to know who he was talking to. I once talked to him for the best part of an hour before he seemed to recognize me!

Little is generally know of the fortitude and courage of Boris Karloff in the face of the physical handicaps he suffered during the last years of his life or his of determination to continue working for as long as he possibly could; as long, as he put it, 'as people want me I feel an obligation to go on performing.' He was pushed in a wheelchair through his last four films, during the two before that he was in a wheelchair most of the time and latterly the oxygen was never far away. Many workers on these films found it a heart-rending sight, but nobody forced him to do it. For years he had said that he would die working and he did his level best to work right up to the end and he enjoyed all of it, particularly *The Incredible Invasion* where, as a malevolent scientist, he worked on the laboratory set that had been used in *Frankenstein* and *Bride of Frankenstein*.

Perhaps as well as anyone Boris Karloff appreciated and succeeded so often in satisfying a need that seems to be inside us all; a constant and ever-present yearning for the fantastic, for the darkly mysterious and for the cloaked terror of the dark. This need is sometimes satisfied by religion, sometimes by superstition, but perhaps most healthily by escapist tales of terror.

It could be said that he died, as he always hoped he would, in harness although he was ill through much of 1968 and was admitted to the King Edward VII Hospital, Midhurst, Sussex in the November of that year. He died there on 2nd February 1969, in his eighty-second year, and at Guildford cremation was arranged to take place as soon as possible after death and as quietly as possible; in fact the Crematorium Superintendent tells me that only four people were present at the funeral on 5th February 1969. The ashes were buried in the lawn of the Garden of Remembrance, where, at the time of writing, no permanent memorial has been erected to his memory. He died, one of only two or three actors to have declined to send a biographical note to *Who's Who in the Theatre*, and as incurably stage-struck as he had been when he played the Demon King in a church pantomime seventy years before.

Select Bibliography

(Place of publication is London unless stated otherwise)

Agee on Film by James Agee. USA, 1958.
And the Darkness Falls. Edited by Boris Karloff. USA, 1946.
The Boris Karloff Horror Anthology. Edited by Boris Karloff. 1965.
Champagne and Chandeliers by Charles Graves. 1958.
Costumes by Nathan by Archie Nathan. 1960.
Current Biography 1941 Who's Who and Why. USA, 1941.
Drawn and Quartered by Charles Addams. USA, 1942.
Film Pictorial Annual, 1938.
The Film Till Now by Paul Rotha. 1949.
Foremost Films of 1938 by Frank Vreeland. USA, 1939.
Frankenstein by Mary Shelley. 1818, etc.
Ghost Writer by Fred Archer. 1966.
Hadn't We the Gaiety? by John Paddy Carstairs. 1945.
Histoire du Cinéma Americain by Pierre Artis. Paris, 1947.
The History of the British Film 1914–1918 by Rachael Low. 1950.
Hollywood in the Thirties by John Baxter. 1968.
Horror Movies by Carlos Clarens. 1968.
Horrors by Drake Douglas. 1967.
The Last Man by Mary Shelley. 1826.
The Lion's Share by Bosley Crowther. USA, 1957.

Mary Shelley by Eileen Bigland. 1959.
The Movies by Richard Griffith and Arthur Mayer. 1957.
The Movies, Mr Griffiths and Me by Lillian Gish. 1969.
The Parade's Gone By by Kevin Brownlow. 1968.
Pictorial History of Hollywood Film Monsters by Brad Steiger. USA, 1965.
A Pictorial History of the Movies by Deems Taylor. 1951.
Register of Merchant Taylors' School. Edited by E P Hart. 1936.
Seventy Years of Cinema by Peter Cowie. 1969.
Stars of the Screen. Compiled by J S Ross. 1934.
Tales of Terror. Edited by Boris Karloff. USA, 1943.
This Was Hollywood by Beth Day. 1960.
Two Reels and a Crank by Albert E Smith. USA, 1952.
Wonder Album of Filmland. Edited by Clarence Winchester. 1933.

Periodicals: *The Bookseller; Christian Science Monitor; Daily Sketch; Films and Filming; Film Weekly; Good Housekeeping; New York Herald Tribune; New York Times; Picturegoer; The Times; Daily Cinema; Film Review* (USA); *Kinematograph Weekly; Monthly Film Bulletin; Financial Times; Newsreel* (USA); *TV Times; Films in Review* (USA); *Screen Facts* (USA); *Cinema* (Britain); *Celuloids* (Portugal); *Cinema Today; Weekly Cinema; Saturday Review; The People; The Daily Telegraph; The Guardian; Sunday Express.*

Discography of Recordings made by Boris Karloff for Caedmon Records

Boris Karloff and Lewis Casson recounting the revelries of Mr Pickwick's Christmas and the ghostly tale of *The Goblins Who Stole a Sexton*.   TC 1121.

Boris Karloff and four other actors read poems by Rudyard Kipling.   TC 1193.

Boris Karloff and eight other actors read 'Classics of English Poetry'.   TC 1301.

Boris Karloff reads *Petunia, Beware!* by Roger Duvoisin, and *The Pony Engine* by Doris Garn. (Coupled with Julie Harris reading two other stories.)   TC 1182.

Boris Karloff, with Cyril Ritchard and Celeste Holm, in *Mother Goose*.   TC 1091.

Boris Karloff reads *The Three Little Pigs*, *The Three Bears*, *Jack and the Beanstalk*, *The Old Woman and Her Pig*, *Henny Penny*, *Hereafterthis*, *The Three Sillies*, and *King of the Cats*.   TC 1129.

Boris Karloff reads fifty of Aesop's Fables including *The Fox and the Grapes*, *The Goose with the Golden Eggs*, and *The Hare and the Tortoise*.   TC 1221.

Boris Karloff reads *The Little Match Girl, Thumbelina, The Swineherd, The Top and the Ball,* and *The Red Shoes.*
TC 1117.

Boris Karloff reads *The Ugly Duckling, The Shepherdess and the Chimney-Sweep, The Princess and the Pea, The Collar, Clod-Poll,* and *The Fir Tree.* TC 1109.

Boris Karloff reads *The Hunting of the Snark* by Lewis Carroll and *The Pied Piper* by Robert Browning.
TC 1075.

Boris Karloff reads *The Reluctant Dragon* by Kenneth Grahame. TC 1074.

Boris Karloff reads *Just So Stories* by Rudyard Kipling: *How the Whale Got His Throat, How the Camel Got His Hump, How the Rhinoceros Got His Skin.* Also *Mowgli's Brothers* from *The Jungle Book.* TC 1038*.

Boris Karloff reads *More Just So Stories* by Rudyard Kipling: *The Elephant's Child, The Sing-Song of Old Man Kangeroo, The Beginning of the Armadillos, How the Leopard Got His Spots.* TC 1088.

Boris Karloff reads *Other Just So Stories* by Rudyard Kipling: *The Cat That Walked by Herself, The Butterfly That Stamped, How the First Letter Was Written.* TC 1139.

Boris Karloff reads *The Jungle Book* by Rudyard Kipling: *How Fear Came.* TC 1100.

Boris Karloff reads *The Jungle Book* by Rudyard Kipling: *Toomai of the Elephants.* TC 1176.

Boris Karloff as the King of Britain with Claire Bloom and Pamela Brown in *Cymbeline* by William Shakespeare.
SRS 236.

Appendix

A chronological record of
the films in which
Boris Karloff
appeared with outline of screenplay,
cast, year of release
and technical details of
many of the more important
films.

APPENDIX

The Films of Boris Karloff

BORIS KARLOFF APPEARED in over 160 films and this is the first comprehensive and chronological list to be published. An outline of the screenplay, where available, has been included where this does not appear in the text of this work, together with details of cast, producing team and company and other technical details. While I am indebted to the British Film Institute Research Department and Westminster Reference Library for making their archives readily available, I assume sole responsibility for any errors or omissions for which I apologise in advance. Notification of any mistakes will be gratefully acknowledged.

1916 *The Dumb Girl of Portici* Universal Director: Max Ratinoff. With Anna Pavlova, Lois Weber, Douglas Gerrard. A vehicle for the great Russian prima-ballerina.

1919 *The Lightning Raider* Pathe Director: George B Seitz. With Pearl White, Warner Oland, Henry G Sell. A 15-part serial based on stories by May Yohe, adapted by Charles Goddard and John B Clymer.

1919 *The Masked Raider* Arrow (releasing company) Director: Aubrey M Kennedy. With Harry Myers, Ruth Stonehouse, Paul Panzer. A 15-part serial.

1919 *His Majesty, the American* UA Director: Joseph Henabery. With Douglas Fairbanks Snr, Lillian Langdon, Marjorie Daw. Karloff as a spy in a mythical European kingdom. One of the best of Henabery's early pictures.

1920 *The Prince and Betty* Pathe Director: Robert Thornby. With William Desmond, as the long-lost heir to the kingdom of Mervo. Karloff had a bit part.

1920 *The Deadlier Sex* Pathe Director: Robert Thornby. With Blanche Sweet, Mahlon Hamilton. Karloff noticeable as a French-Canadian trapper who fights the hero.

1920 *The Courage of Marge O'Doone* Vitagraph Director: David Smith. With Pauline Starke, Jack Curtis, Miles Welch, William Dyer. Karloff as a trapper who kidnaps the infant Marge.

1920 *The Last of the Mohicans* Associated Producers (their first production) Director: Maurice Tourneur. With Wallace Beery, Barbara Bedford, Lillian Hall, Albert Roscol, Harry Lorraine. From the famous novel by James Fenimore Cooper, with Beery as the evil Magua and Karloff as one of his band. Made on location at Big Bear Lake and Yosemite Valley with striking lighting effects and weather atmosphere.

1921 *The Romance of the Hope Diamond* Kleine Films Director: Stuart Patron. (Entitled *The Hope Diamond Mystery* in USA.) With Harry Carter,

George Cheseboro, Grace Darmond, William Marion, Boris Karloff. A 15-part serial with Karloff the villain.

1921 *Without Benefit of Clergy* Pathe Director: James Young. With Virginia Brown Faire. From the novel by Rudyard Kipling, with Karloff as the villain, Ahmed Khan.

1921 *Cheated Hearts* Universal Director: Hobart Henley. With Herbert Rawlinson, Warner Baxter, Marjorie Daw. Karloff had the part of a Mexican bandit.

1922 *The Cave Girl* First National Director: Joseph J Franz. With Teddie Gerard. Karloff was a villainous halfbreed who kidnapped the heroine and abducted her in a canoe.

1922 *The Altar Stairs* Universal Director: Lambert Hillyer. With Frank Mayo. An adventure film set in the South Seas.

1922 *The Infidel* First National Director: James Young. With Katherine MacDonald and Robert Ellis. Karloff played the ruler of a fictitious Menang island who orders the massacre of the white settlers.

1922 *Omar, the Tentmaker* First National Director: James Young. With Guy Bates Post, Virginia Brown Faire, Patsy Ruth Miller, Noah Beery Snr. A melodrama set in Old Baghdad with Karloff in his first sympathetic role.

1922 *Nan of the North* Arrow (releasing company) Director: Duke Worne. With Ann Little, Leonard Clapham, Joseph W Girard.

1922 *The Man from Downing Street* Vitagraph Director:

Edward Jose. A spy story with Karloff as a Maharajah.

1922 *A Woman Conquers* First National Director: Tom Forman. With Katherine MacDonald, Bryant Washburn. Karloff as a French-Canadian trapper in another 'northwoods' story.

1923 *The Prisoner* Universal Director: Jack Conway. With Herbert Rawlinson. A romantic melodrama in an Austrian setting with Karloff in a small role. This film was included in Sherwood's *Best Movie Pictures of 1922-1923*.

1924 *Riders of the Plains* Arrow (releasing company) Director: Jacques Jaccard. With Jack Perrin, Marilyn Mills, Ruth Royce. A 15-part serial.

1924 *Dynamite Dan* Sunset Pictures Director: Bruce Mitchell. With Kenneth MacDonald. A boxing story with Karloff as the villain. Karloff's best part to date.

1925 *Perils of the Wind* Universal Director: Francis Ford. With Joe Bonomo, Margaret Quimby, Jack Mower. A 15-part serial.

1925 *Prairie Wife* MGM Director: Hugo Ballin. With Dorothy Devone, Herbert Rawlinson, Gibson Gowland. Karloff's first real Western; he played a Mexican halfbreed.

1925 *Forbidden Cargo* FBO/RC Pictures Director: Tom Buckingham. With Evelyn Brent. Karloff was the mate on Brent's rum-smuggling ship.

1925 *Lady Robin Hood* FBO/RC Pictures Director: Ralph Ince. With Evelyn Brent, Robert Ellis. Karloff was an evil governor against revolutionist Brent, aided by Ellis.

1925 *Parisian Nights*   FBO/RC Pictures   Director: Alfred Santell. With Helene Hammerstein, Lou Tellegen, Renee Adoree, Gaston Glass and Karloff as the Parisian *apache*. This was Alfred Santell's first long film and his assistant was Robert Florey. The film was shot in three weeks with the outside scenes photographed at San Francisco. The sombre story was created by Emil Forst, a former officer in the Austrian army who later committed suicide. The story, set in La Chapelle, concerned the rivalry between two gangs: Tellegen's 'Wolves' and Karloff's 'Panthers'. During the course of one fight Tellegen thrust a knife under the nose of Karloff who fainted at the sight of the blade!

1925 *Never the Twain Shall Meet*   MGM   Director: Maurice Tourneur. With Anita Stewart, Bert Lytell, Huntley Gordon. A South Sea Island story with Karloff as one of the villains. Reissued in 1931.

1926 *The Greater Glory*   First National   Director: Curt Rehfeld. With Anna Q Nilsson, Conway Tearle, May Allison, Ian Keith, Lucy Beaumont, Jean Hersholt and Boris Karloff as a scissors-grinder in a story of Vienna during the First World War.

1926 *The Bells*   Chadwick Pictures   Director: James Young. Screenplay by James Young. Based on the play by Erckmann-Chatrian. With Lionel Barrymore, Eddie Phillips, Lola Todd, Fred Warren, Boris Karloff, Gustav von Seyffertitz, Otto Lederer, Lorimer Johnston. The famous Henry Irving stage success; Karloff had the part of the mesmerist, his best role to date; Barrymore was the murderer.

1926 *Eagle of the Sea*   Paramount   Director: Frank Lloyd.

With Ricardo Cortez, Florence Vidor. Karloff
played a scurvy-looking member of the crew of
pirate Jean Lafitte (Cortez). Florence Vidor's
serene beauty made her a long-time favourite.
Ricardo Cortez was challenging Rudolf
Valentino as a dashing Latin lover.

1926 *Old Ironsides* Paramount Director: James Cruze.
With Charles Farrell, Esther Ralston, Wallace
Beery, George Bancroft. Karloff was a Barbary
pirate.

1926 *Flames* Associated Exhibitors Director: Lewis H
Moomaw. With Eugene O'Brien, Virginia Valli,
Jean Hersholt, Bryant Washburn. Karloff as bandit
Blackie Blanchette in a railroad story.

1926 *The Golden Webb* Gotham Director: Walter Lang.
With Lillian Rich, Huntley Gordon and Karloff as
a deserving victim in a murder mystery.

1926 *Phantoms of the Bat.*

1926 *Flaming Fury* FBO/RC Pictures Director: James P
Hogan.

1926 *Her Honour, The Governor* FBO/RC Pictures
Director: Chet Withey. Photography by Andre
Balatier. With Carroll Nye, Pauline Frederick,
Greta von Rue, Tom Santschi. Karloff had the
part of Snipe Collins, a fiendish crook, in this
story of political corruption.

1926 *The Man in the Saddle* Universal Director: Clifford
S Smith. With Hoot Gibson and Fay Wray. Hoot
Gibson solves a series of Western hotel robberies
perpetrated by Karloff.

1926 *The Nickel Hopper* Pathe A Hal Roach Comedy.
3-reeler. With Mabel Normand, Theodore van Eltz

and both Oliver Hardy and Boris Karloff in small parts. Karloff, a seedy roué who tries to pick up Mabel Normand at a dance hall, had some good close-ups and showed a neat sense of comic menace.

1927 *Tarzan and the Golden Lion* FBO/RC Pictures Director: J P McGowan. Based on stories by Edgar Rice Burroughs. With James H Pierce as Tarzan against lion-worshippers; Edna Murphy played Ruth Burton and Karloff had a supporting role.

1927 *Let it Rain* Paramount Director: Eddie Cline. With Douglas MacLean, Shirly Mason, Wade Butler. A comedy, with plenty of action, about the Marines.

1927 *The Meddlin' Stranger* Pathe Director: Richard Thorpe. With Wally Wales. A Western with Karloff as one of the main villains.

1927 *Princess from Hoboken* Tiffany Director: Allan Dale.

1927 *The Phantom Buster* Pathe Director: William Bertram. With Buddy Roosevelt. A Western with Karloff as a border smuggler.

1927 *Soft Cushions* Paramount Director: Eddie Cline. With Douglas MacLean, Sue Carol, Richard Carle, Tussel Powell. Karloff played the chief conspirator in this 'Arabian Nights' comedy.

1927 *Two Arabian Knights* United Artists Director: Lewis Milestone. Screenplay by James O'Donohue and Wallace Smith. With William Boyd, Louis Wolheim, Mary Astor, Ian Keith, Michael Vavitch, DeWitt Jennings, Michael Visaroff, Boris Karloff. Karloff was the ship's purser in this Rabelaisian satire on life in the army.

1927 *The Love Mart* First National Director: George Fitzmaurice. With Gilbert Roland, Billie Dove, Raymond Turner, Noah Beery, Boris Karloff. Karloff had the part of Fleming in this well-produced swashbuckling story of old New Orleans.

1928 *The Vanishing Rider* Universal Director: Ray Taylor. With William Desmond, Ethlyne Clair, Bud Osborne, Nelson McDowell. A 10-part serial.

1928 *Vultures of the Sea* Mascot Director: Richard Thorpe. With Johnnie Walker, Shirley Mason, Tom Santschi, Boris Karloff. A 10-part serial.

1928 *Burning the Wind* Universal Directors: Henry McRea and Herbert Blanche. With Hoot Gibson, Virginia Brown Faire. Karloff as a wicked ranch foreman who kidnaps the heroine.

1929 *Little Wild Girl* Trinity Director: Frank S Mattison. With Lila Lee, Cullen Landis, Frank Merrill, Sheldon Lewis and Boris Karloff as Maurice Kent, the villain, in another 'northwoods' drama.

1929 *The Devil's Chaplain* Rayart Director: Duke Worne. With Josef Swickard, Virginia Brown Faire, Cornelius Keefe, Wheeler Oakman and Boris Karloff as 'Boris', a small part in this spy story.

1929 *Phantoms of the North* Biltmore Productions Director: Henry Webb. With Donald Keith, Edith Roberts, Boris Karloff. Another 'northwoods' story with Karloff as a murderer.

1929 *Two Sisters* Rayart Director: Scott Pembroke. With Viola Dana, Rex Lease, Clair Du Brey, Irving Bacon and Karloff as Cecil, henchman to

Viola Dana, who had a dual role, when she is a crook. Story by Virginia Terhune Vandewater.

1929 *Behind that Curtain* Fox Director: Irving Cummings. Screenplay by Sonya Levien and Clark Silvernail, from the novel by Earl Derr Biggers. Cert. 'A'. With Warner Baxter, Lois Moran, Gilbert Emery, Claud King, Montague Shaw and Boris Karloff as 'Karlov' in a 'Charlie Chan' murder mystery although Chan (E L Park) had only a small part.

1929 *The Unholy Night* MGM Director: Lionel Barrymore. Screenplay by Dorothy Farnum and Edwin Justus Mayer from a story by Ben Hecht. Cert. 'A'. With Ernest Torrence, Dorothy Sebastian, Roland Young, Nathalie Moorehead, Polly Moran, Sojin, Sidney Jarvis, George Cooper, John Milyan, Boris Karloff, John Loder. This good thriller, set in London, saw Karloff as a Hindu servant in his first sound picture.

1929 *King of the Kongo* Mascot Director: Richard Thorpe. With Jacqueline Logan, Walter Miller, Richard Tucker. Karloff, the apparent villain, turns out to be the heroine's father. A 16-part serial, released in two versions – silent and sound, the latter with synchronised musical score, sound effects and dialogue.

1929 *The Fatal Warning* Mascot Director: Richard Thorpe. With Helen Costello, Ralph Graves, Syd Crossley, George Periolat, Phillip Smalley, Lloyd Whitlock, Boris Karloff. Ten 2-reel episodes.

1930 *The Bad One* United Artists/Schenck Director: George Fitzmaurice. Cert. 'A'. With Dolores Del

Rio, Edmund Lowe, Don Alvarado, Ullrich Haupt. Lowe kills a rival for Dolores Del Rio and serves his sentence on a penal colony where Karloff is a guard under a sadistic overseer.

1930 *The Sea Bat* MGM Director: Wesley Ruggles. Cert. 'U'. With Raquel Torres, Charles Bickford, Nils Asther, George F Marion and Boris Karloff as a villainous halfbreed. Charles Bickford was a Devil's Island escapee.

1930 *The Utah Kid* Tiffany Director: Richard Thorpc. With Rex Lease, Tom Santschi, Dorothy Sebastian. Karloff, in his last old-type Western, played a bandit.

1930 *Mothers Cry* Warner Brothers Director: Hobart Henley. With Dorothy Peterson, Helen Chandler, David Manners, Evalyn Knapp, Ed Woods. The story of a bad son paying the death penalty in spite of his mother's love. Karloff was a murder victim.

1931 *King of the Wild* Mascot Director: Reeves Eason. With Walter Miller, Nora Lane, Dorothy Christie, Tom Santschi, Boris Karloff, Carroll Nye. Karloff was a villainous sheik with a phony French accent in this story of the terrible experiences of a young American who escapes from an Indian prison. Twelve 2-reel episodes. Issued as a full-length film in Argentina in 1933 as *Bimi*.

1931 *The Criminal Code* Colombia Director: Howard Hawks. Cert. 'A'. With Walter Huston, Phillips Holmes, Constance Cummings, Boris Karloff. An unusual picture with Walter Huston giving a strong, rugged characterisation as a warden of a prison, whose Bible is his law. As district attorney he had convicted many of the prisoners. The picture succeeded in laying bare the soul of a prisoner who is a victim of circumstances rather than a confirmed criminal, and prison life was depicted in all its brutality and soul-destroying aspects. Karloff repeated his stage success as a 'trusty' who kills a 'stool-pigeon'.

1931 *Cracked Nuts* RKO Director: Edward Cline. Cert. 'U'. With Bert Wheeler, Robert Woolsey, Edna May Oliver, Dorothy Lee, Stanley Fields, Boris Karloff. An elaborate and humorous extravaganza with Karloff as a revolutionist in the kingdom of El Dorania.

1931 *Young Donovan's Kid* RKO Director: Fred Niblo. With Richard Dix, Jackie Cooper, Marion Shilling, Frank Sheridan. Richard Dix was a racketeer who tries to bring up orphan Jackie Cooper, the son of a fellow gangster. Karloff was the dope-peddler.

1931 *Smart Money* Warners Director: Alfred E Green. Cert. 'A'. With Edward G Robinson, James Cagney, Evalyn Knapp, Joan Blondell. The story of a small-town barber who becomes a big-time gambler and loses all his friends' money. Karloff was a crooked gambler who tries to cheat the one-time barber, Robinson; Cagney was Robinson's gangland partner.

1931 *The Public Defender* RKO Director: J Walter Ruben. Cert. 'U'. With Richard Dix, Shirley Grey, Edmund Breese, Paul Hurst, Nella Walker. From the novel *The Splendid Crime* by George Goodchild. A modern crook drama with Dix as

'The Reckoner' and Karloff as his cultured accomplice.

1931 *Business and Pleasure* Fox Director: David Butler. Cert. 'U'. With Will Rogers, Jetta Goudal, Joel McCrea, Dorothy Peterson. From the play *The Plutocrat* by Arthur Goodrich, based on a novel by Booth Tarkington. The story of a magnate who goes to the East to obtain the secret of making Damascus steel. Rogers was a razorblade king from Oklahoma; Karloff a sheik.

1931 *I Like Your Nerve* First National Director: William McGann. Cert. 'U'. With Loretta Young, Douglas Fairbanks Jnr, Henry Kolker, Claud Allister, Paul Porcasi, Ivan Simpson, Edmund Brecon. From a story by Ronald Pertwee. A rather slight comedy-adventure story of a young man who falls in love with the step-daughter of a dignitary of a South American state, which was helped by a very good supporting cast including Karloff as a butler.

1931 *Five Star Final* First National Director: Mervyn LeRoy. Adapted from the play by Louis Weitzenkorn. Cert. 'A'. With Edward G Robinson, H N Warner, Marian Marsh, Aline MacMahon, Anthony Bushell, George E Stone, Frances Starr, Ona Musan, Boris Karloff. A fine film which exposed the heartless manner in which an American newspaper proprietor seeks to boost his circulation by publishing a long-dead scandal which has the effect of driving two young people to suicide and ruining a young girl's life. Robinson was the unscrupulous editor and Karloff his evil assistant,

Isopod, who among other pursuits, was a vicious fake clergyman.

1931 *The Mad Genius* Warners Director: Michael Curtiz. Screenplay by J Grubb Alexander and Harvey Thew from the play *The Idol* by Martin Brown. Cert. 'A'. With John Barrymore, Marian Marsh, Charles Butterworth, Carmel Myens, Donald Cook, Boris Karloff. Boris Karloff played a clubfoot man who was passionately fond of dancing. Unable to perform himself, he poured all his genius into his adopted son, Fedor, (John Barrymore). Fedor becomes famous and falls in love with Nana (Marian Marsh), a girl in the ballet. Fearing this will ruin his career, his father exercises his strange hypnotic influence over him and resorts to any trick to keep the lovers apart. Eventually he is killed by a madman during the performance of a ballet, and Fedor and Nana find the happiness they have sought. A curious film, rather reminiscent of Barrymore's *Svengali*.

1931 *The Guilty Generation* Columbia Director: Rowland V Lee. Cert. 'A'. With Leo Carillo, Constance Cummings, Robert Young, Boris Karloff, Emma Dunn, Leslie Fenton. From the play by Jo Milward and J Kirby Hawkes, this is a story of Italian-American gangsterism; one of the earliest films to get away from whitewashing racketeers and showing gangsters in their true colours. In the picture no sympathy was accorded to the members of the two rival gangs; in fact they were shown in a very unfavourable light. Leo Carillo gave a most interesting study of an Italian-American racketeer who does not hesitate to contemplate the murder of his son-in-law to get level with his rivals. Finally his mother takes a hand and kills her own son in order to save further bloodshed. It was strong fare but very dramatically put over and there were many thrills and well-acted sequences. Karloff and Carillo were rival beer barons; Young was Karloff's son.

1931 *The Yellow Passport* Fox Director: Raoul Walsh. From the play by Michael Morton. Cert. 'A.' (*The Yellow Ticket* in USA.) A remake of a silent film. With Elissa Landi, Lionel Barrymore, Laurence Olivier, Walter Byron, Sarah Padder, Arnold Koeff, Mischer Auer, Boris Karloff. A social melodrama set in Russia in 1913 concerning a girl (Elissa Landi), who, to enable her to visit her father imprisoned on a political charge, obtains a signed yellow-ticket which are only issued to women of a 'certain class'. She eventually reaches the cell containing her father – to find him dead. She becomes embroiled in officialdom when she attempts to show up the whole grisly oppression. A Czarist official (Lionel Barrymore) tries to seduce her but is thwarted by a young English journalist (Laurence Olivier). Boris Karloff had the small part of Barrymore's orderly.

1931 *Graft* Universal Director: Christy Cabanne. Cert. 'U.' With Regis Toomey, Sue Carol, Dorothy Revier, Boris Karloff. A brisk newspaper drama, perhaps more melodramatic than realistic, dealing with the misfortunes and troubles of a newspaper reporter, put across in such a distinctive manner that the filmgoer sympathises with him in his difficulties. Toomey was the reporter who trailed a murderer (Karloff) to a yacht and finally brings him to justice.

1931 *Dirigible* Columbia Director: Frank Capra. Cert. 'A'. From a story by Lt Commander F W Wead. With Jack Holt, Ralph Graves, Fay Wray, Hobart Bosworth. An authentic and thrilling story of an air expedition to the South Pole by means of 'modern' aircraft including the airship 'Los Angeles'. There were exciting moments, as when an aeroplane is hooked to the keel of the airship and when a fleet of nonrigid airships fill the screen. The atmosphere was well portrayed with the awful quiet and the endless whiteness of the polar region, in which some members of the exploration team perish; including Boris Karloff.

1931 *The Last Parade* United Artists Director: Erle C Kenton, Cert. 'A'. With Jack Holt, Tim Moore, Constance Cummings. The story of a wisecracking reporter (Jack Holt) returning to America from the First World War to find his job given to a younger man. After many disappointments he takes to driving liquor trucks for an oily czar of a racketeer and soon finds himself prosperous and with a notorious reputation. When a girlfriend's brother publishes news items about his activities the racketeer has him killed, and is in turn killed by the hero who is sentenced to death, but owing to the pleas of the girl there are hopes that he will receive a pardon. Karloff played the part of a prison warder.

1931 *Frankenstein* Universal Director: James Whale. Screenplay by Garrett Fort, Francis Edward Farugoh and Robert Florey from the play by Peggy Webling based on the book by Mary Shelley. Cert. 'A'. The horror classic that catapulted Karloff to international fame. With Colin Clive, Mae Clarke, John Boles, Boris Karloff, Edward Von Sloan, Dwight Frye, Frederick Kerr, Lionel Belmore. A 'horror-shocker' concerning a German scientist who discovers how to create life out of dead tissues. He makes a monster in the likeness of a man. The monster commits two murders and all but kills his creator, but is finally destroyed in a blazing mill, the scientist recovering to marry his loved one. The monster, with its loneliness, its hysterical fear of fire, and its strange, compelling eyes, was not without a peculiar pathos. Reissued, 1938.

1931 *Tonight or Never* Production: Feature Productions Distributor: United Artists. Director: Mervyn LeRoy. Cert. 'A'. Specially written for the screen by Ernest Vadja from the David Belasco stage success, with Gloria Swanson, Melvyn Douglas, Ferdinand Gottschalk, Boris Karloff. The story of a temperamental prima-donna, who is made to fall in love with a man she imagines to be a *gigolo* kept by a rich *marchesa*, but who in fact turns out to be an impresario. Boris Karloff was noticeable as the waiter; he had one very funny scene with Melvyn Douglas.

1932 *Alias the Doctor* Warners Director: Michael Curtiz. With Richard Barthelmess, Marian Marsh,

Lucille La Varne, Norman Foster. Karloff as the malevolent autopsy surgeon. Barthelmess sacrifices his medical career for a no-good brother and later practices without a licence.

1932 *Cohens and the Kellys in Hollywood* Universal Director: John Francis Dillon. With George Sidney, Charles Murray, June Clyde, Norman Foster. A film, not released in Britain, of a series about two families. This time they meet Karloff, playing himself, at a restaurant. The films featured the famous American comedy team of George Sidney and Charles Murray.

1932 *The Miracle Man* Paramount Director: Norman Z McLeod. Cert. 'A'. From the story by Lucius Packard and Robert E Davis and the play by George M Cohan. With John Wray, Sylvia Sidney, Chester Morris, Irving Pichel, Hobart Bosworth, Boris Karloff. The story of three men and a girl who are reformed by the influence of a faith-healer whom they sought to exploit. A remake of the fine 1919 silent film; Wray had Lon Chaney's part and Karloff was Nikko, a shrewd charlatan who runs a fake mission.

1932 *Behind the Mask* Columbia Director: John Francis Dillon. Cert. 'A'. Adapted from *In the Secret Service*. Jack Holt, Constance Cummings, Boris Karloff. A mystery thriller about a member of the Secret Service (Jack Holt) who discovers the leader of a narcotics ring (Boris Karloff), who has a habit of putting all those who cross his path out of the way in a peculiarly unpleasant manner.

1932 *The Mummy* Universal Director: Karl Freund.

Cert. 'A'. Screenplay by John L Balderston based on a story by Nina Wilcox Putnam and Richard Schayer. Photography: Charles Stumar. With Boris Karloff, Zita Johann, David Manners, Edward Van Sloan, Arthur Byron, Bramwell Fletcher. First and best of the Mummy films. A genuine thriller in which a mummy comes to life; the reincarnation is an exceptionally good piece of cinema – and camera technique. Karloff is a prince in ancient Egypt who violates the tomb of an Egyptian princess he was in love with and comes back from the dead to claim a modern girl as the reincarnated princess.

1932 *The Old Dark House* Universal Director: James Whale. Cert. 'A'. Screenplay by Ben W Levy from the novel *Benighted* by J B Priestley. Dialogue by R C Sherriff. Distributed by General Films. With Boris Karloff, Melvyn Douglas, Charles Laughton, Gloria Stuart, Lilian Bond, Ernest Thesiger, Raymond Massey. Reissued, 1945. A thriller about five travellers who, lost in a violent storm at night, take refuge in a sinister old house inhabited by a nightmarish family including a bedridden centenarian father with a wicked past, a viciously righteous old daughter, and two sons, one an ineffective, brittle coward (Ernest Thesiger), the other a madman who is looked after by an incredible brute of a dumb, but homicidal, butler (Boris Karloff). The butler gets drunk, attacks one of the women travellers, and then lets out the mad son, who is killed in a fight with one of the men travellers (Melvyn Douglas). The film ends happily with this traveller becoming engaged to a chorus-girl who is another of the shelterers in the house with her protector (Charles Laughton). Excellent camera-work by Arthur Edeson.

1932 *Night World* Universal Director: Hobart Henley. Cert. 'A'. With Lew Ayres, Mae Clarke, Boris Karloff, Dorothy Revier. Several stories were woven into this tale which attempted to show the romance and drama which lurk in the hectic atmosphere of a nightclub. Boris Karloff as the nightclub proprietor – without fantastic make-up – had a sympathetic role.

1932 *The Mask of Fu Manchu* MGM Directors: Charles Brabin and Charles Vidor. Cert. 'A'. From stories by Sax Rohmer. With Boris Karloff, Lewis Stone, Karen Morley, Charles Starrett, Myrna Loy, Jean Hersholt. An oriental mystery with a somewhat fantastic and hectic plot, which is kept going at a tremendous pace with lurid action in the torture chambers ... Boris Karloff is a sinister Dr Fu Manchu and Lewis Stone a convincing Nayland Smith. In this film Fu Manchu steals a mask of Genghis Khan from the British Museum in order to start a 'holy war'; when the museum officials come for it, he commits the usual Fu Manchu tortures.

1932 *Scarface* United Artists Director: Howard Hawks. Cert. 'A'. With Paul Muni, George Raft, Karen Morley, Ann Dvorak, Boris Karloff. A gangster story set in Prohibition America and showing the bitter and relentless warfare that was waged between rival gangs. While the police seem helpless the activities of the gangs become more and more daring; for one gang to impinge on another's territory is sufficient to provoke immediate and murderous retaliation. After each exploit the principal gang leader returns to his steel-shuttered, bullet-proof flat. The final scenes between the gangs and the police are a terrific *melée* in which machine guns and gas play the leading parts. Finally, his courage having deserted him, the gang leader screams with terror as the police overpower him. Generally regarded as one of the best gangster films ever made with the characters portrayed as real people, seen in the round. Karloff was a gang leader. *Scarface* was reissued in 1938. The film was also shown in America as *Scar on the Nation*.

1933 *The Ghoul* Gaumont-British Director: T Hayes Hunter. Cert 'A'. With Boris Karloff, Cedric Hardwicke, Ernest Thesiger, Dorothy Hyson, Anthony Bushell. An exciting (British) film set in an eerie country mansion with Boris Karloff in the dual-role of a half-mad recluse and a master criminal. After being buried alive Karloff returns to search for a priceless jewel which has been stolen from him, killing a few people before his own demise.

1933 *Mickey's Gala Premiere* Walt Disney Boris Karloff, Bela Lugosi, and Lon Chaney appeared in cartoon form.

1934 *The House of Doom* Universal Director: Edgar G Ulmer. Screenplay by Peter Rurie. Producer: E M Asher. Photography: John Mescall. Cert 'A'. With Boris Karloff, Bela Lugosi, David Manners,

Jacqueline Wells, Lucille Lund, Egon Brecher and John Carradine. A newly married couple meet a sinister stranger (Bela Lugosi) on the Continental Express and they continue their journey with him in a motor coach. When the coach crashes the stranger takes them to the house of a friend where strange happenings alarm the young couple. The stranger and his host are then revealed as deadly enemies. The girl is soon in danger from the evil host (Boris Karloff), but is saved by the stranger who allows the pair to escape before blowing up the house. Designated by the Board of Censors as a 'Horror' film. (Entitled *The Black Cat* in USA, where it was re-released in 1951 as *The Vanishing Body*.)

1934 *Gift of Gab* Universal Director: Karl Freund. Cert. 'A'. From a story by Jerry Wald and Phil G Epstein. With Edmund Lowe, Gloria Stuart, Ruth Etting, Paul Lucas. Edmund Lowe played a 'show-off' announcer in the early days of radio, introducing famous stars who made brief appearances – including Boris Karloff.

1934 *The Lost Patrol* RKO Director: John Ford. Cert. 'A'. From a novel by Philip MacDonald. With Victor McLaglen, Boris Karloff, Reginald Denny, Wallace Ford, Alan Hale, J M Kerrigan, Billy Bevan, Brandon Hurst. A British patrol from the army in Mesopotamia is lost among the sandhills; their officer is picked off by an Arab sniper and the sergeant takes command. Without knowing either their instructions or their whereabouts, they encamp at an oasis and there have to endure the vigilance of unseen enemies who pick them off singly as opportunity occurs. A virile but harrowing tale told without embellishments, giving a very real sense of the solitude and bleakness of the desert. Karloff was superb as the insane religious fanatic. Reissued in 1949.

1934 *The House of Rothschild* 20th-Century Fox Director: Alfred Werker. Distribution: United Artists. Cert. 'U'. With George Arliss, Florence Arliss, Robert Young, Loretta Young, C Aubrey Smith, Boris Karloff. A story written around the rise and progress of the Rothschilds, the famous family of bankers, and their activities during the Napoleonic Wars. Historians criticised the film, but the picture was deeply absorbing and directed with great skill and resourcefulness. Towards the end there was a sequence in Technicolor – a reception by the Prince Regent. George Arliss gave a splendid performance in two parts; Karloff was the anti-Semitic Baron Ledrantz.

1935 *The Black Room* Columbia Director: Roy William Neill. From a screenplay by Henry Myers based on the writings of Arthur Strawn. Cert. 'A'. With Boris Karloff, Marian Marsh, Katherine De Mille, Robert Allen. A period melodrama with fratricide as its theme. Based on a legend that the family of Berghmanns began with twin sons, the elder of whom was murdered by the younger, and will end when history repeats itself and twin boys are born again. Set in Hungary, the film opens with an announcement that twin boys have been born to the family, to the consternation of their father.

Years pass and Grigor, the elder, rules in the castle, hated and feared by his tenants who believe that he seduces and murders their womenfolk. Anton, the younger brother, returning from abroad, is as pleasant and friendly as his brother is sinister and evil. Physically the twins are alike except that Anton has a paralysed arm. Horror is piled on horror as a young peasant girl is thrown into the pit in the Black Room. To calm his infuriated tenants Grigor abdicates in favour of Anton. Then he murders Anton and impersonates him. He makes love to Thea, a beautiful young girl, and murders her father who has discovered his secret. As he is being married to the unwilling Thea, Anton's dogs attack him. In defending himself Grigor uses his right arm, thereby revealing his identity. He flees back to the castle and in an exciting climax the prophesy contained in the legend is fulfilled.

1935 *The Bride of Frankenstein* Universal Director: James Whale. Screenplay by John L Balderston and William Hurlbut. Cert. 'A'. With Boris Karloff, Colin Clive, Elsa Lanchester, Valerie Hobson, Ernest Thesiger, O P Heggie, Dwight Frye, E E Clive, Una O'Connor, John Carradine. A sequel to *Frankenstein* and with a similar theme – the attempt to create life. Beginning where the earlier film ended, the monster escapes from the burning mill, terrifies the countryside, is captured, escapes and finds refuge with a saintly hermit who befriends and teaches him to speak with love and understanding. Meanwhile Dr Frankenstein intends to abandon his experiments and marry. A visit from the sinister Dr Praetorius shakes his determination and the abduction of his fiancée forces him into partnership with the crazy scientist. Their aim is to create a mate for the monster for Praetorius has created life in perfect human form but minute; and he keeps his creations in glass bottles. Frankenstein has been able to create human life full-size but imperfectly. The climax of their collaboration is reached during a terrific storm, when, amid the sizzling and flashing of elaborate electrical apparatus, the swathed form comes to life, only to turn in horror from the being for whom she has been designed as a mate.

1935 *The Raven* Universal Director: Louis Friedlander (Lew Landers). Screenplay by David Boehm. Cert. 'A'. With Boris Karloff, Bela Lugosi, Irene Ware, Lester Matthews. A deliberately horrific film based on some of Poe's *Tales of Mystery and Imagination*, but particularly dwelling on the torture aspects. The story deals with a mad surgeon whose hobby is reconstructing in stone and iron the torture chambers and instruments described by Edgar Allan Poe.

1935 *The Man Who Changed His Mind* Director: Robert Stevenson. Cert. 'A'. (Entitled *The Man Who Lived Again* in USA.) Production: Gainsborough. Distribution: Gaumont-British. With Boris Karloff, Anna Lee, John Loder, Frank Cellier, Lyn Harding, Cecil Parker, Donald Calthrop. Dr Laurience is a scientist who has discovered a method of transferring the whole 'thought-contact'

from one brain to another. When his discoveries
are treated with contempt by the scientific world,
he determines to use them for his own ends, and
to put his own mind into a young and vigorous
body. In order to win the love of his young
laboratory assistant, Clare Wyatt, he puts his own
mind into Dick Haslewood, with whom Clare is in
love. The film was also entitled *Dr Maniac* and *The
Brainsnatcher.*

1936 *Juggernaut* J H Productions Distribution: Twickenham Films. Director: Henry Edwards. Cert. 'A'
With Boris Karloff, Arthur Margetson, Joan
Wyndam, Gibb McLaughlin. Dr Sartoris needs
£20,000 to complete a scientific investigation and
Lady Clifford, second wife of an ailing husband,
wishes to be a rich widow in order to satisfy the
demands of her lover. A bargain is struck and the
doctor gives the husband a fatal injection. But the
dead man's will leaves the lady in the power of
her stepson, Roger, and obviously Roger must now
follow his father. Eve, a young nurse, has her
suspicions, and when Sartoris discovers this he
kidnaps Eve and plans to murder her. However
she escapes just in time to prevent Roger being
injected with tetanus germs and Sartoris commits
a scientific and painful suicide. Meanwhile the
butler, having discovered Lady Clifford putting
poison into Roger's drink, has taken the necessary
steps and serenely ushers out his mistress, struggling, in the grip of the gendarmes, somewhat to
the surprise of the family who are watching the
doctor's death agony in the hall.

1936 *Charlie Chan at the Opera*   20th-Century Fox Director: H Bruce Humberstone. With Warner Oland, Boris Karloff, Charlotte Henry, Keye Luke. Boris Karloff as Gravelle, a former operatic baritone with homicidal tendencies, escapes from an asylum and is suspected of being the culprit in the murder of a tenor. Detective Charlie Chan ultimately succeeds in reaching an entirely satisfactory and unexpected solution which sees Gravelle cured of insanity.

1936 *The Invisible Ray*   Universal   Director: Lambert Hillyer. Screenplay by John Colton from a story by Howard Higgins and Douglas Hodges. Cert. 'A'. With Boris Karloff, Bela Lugosi, Frances Drake, Frank Lawton, Beulah Bondi. While engaged on astronomical research in Africa with Lugosi, Karloff is contaminated by a radioactive meteorite and his slightest touch means death. He kills Lugosi who tries to interfere when Karloff seeks vengeance on Lawton, who is having an affair with Karloff's wife. Ultimately Karloff is himself electrocuted.

1936 *The Walking Dead*   Warner Brothers Distribution: First National. Director: Michael Curtiz. Cert. 'A'. With Boris Karloff, Margeurite Churchill, Richardo Cortez, Edmund Gwenn, Henry O'Neill, Ruth Robinson, Addison Richards, Miki Morita, Eddie Acuff. The story of a man brought back to life after being electrocuted. John Ellerman, an ex-convict, falls into the hands of a group of gangster politicians. They frame him and he is wrongly accused of murdering a judge. Two witnesses of what actually occurred delay too long in coming forward with their testimony and Ellerman is put to death. A doctor succeeds in bringing the body back to life but Ellerman returns a strange, remote being, possessed and obsessed by one idea: to be avenged on his enemies. Relentlessly he pursues his purpose and one by one they meet with violent deaths. When his self-appointed task is finished life once more leaves Ellerman's body.

1937 *Night Key* Universal Distribution: General Films. Director: Lloyd Corrigan. Cert. 'A'. With Boris Karloff, Jean Rogers, Warren Hull, Alan Baxter, Samuel S Hinds. Twenty years previously Mallory (Karloff) was robbed by Ranger (Samuel S Hinds) of his patent rights in a burglar alarm, a device which has since made the latter rich and famous. Today, Mallory, on the verge of blindness, has perfected an invisible ray system which will supersede his earlier invention, and he allows Ranger to cheat him a second time. But he has another instrument up his sleeve, which renders the Ranger Key perfectly useless. Helped by a foolish crook he enters a number of premises protected by the Ranger system and leaves taunting messages behind. A youthful but highly efficient gangster sees that there is money in the idea if only it could be properly developed, and he kidnaps Mallory and forces him to use the device for criminal purposes. Fortunately the scientific equipment of a modern thief's kitchen enables Mallory to turn the tables and eventually bring Ranger to book – though probably on a fifty-fifty basis!

1937 *West of Shanghai* Warner Brothers Distribution: First National. Director: John Farrow. Cert. 'A'. (Entitled *War Lord* in USA). With Boris Karloff, Beverly Roberts, Ricardo Cortez, Gordon Oliver. Jim Hallett has discovered an oilfield in Northern China, in territory overrun by bandit Fang, played by Boris Karloff. Two financiers are in competition for concessions in this field and they travel to nearby Sha Ho Shen. At the missionary station they find one of their estranged wives, who is now in love with the other financier. Suddenly Fang arrives with his band and much parleying is done about ransoms. There is any amount of double-dealing and at length one of the financiers is killed. Finally however, Fang, a good-hearted and high-principled bandit who is loyal to his friends, is killed together with the whole of his gang. The film was largely concerned with showing Fang's nobility and the meanness of the Western financiers.

1938 *The Invisible Menace* Warner Brothers Distribution: First National. Director: John Farrow. Stage play: Ralph Spencer Zink. Screenplay: Crane Wilbur. Cert. 'A'. With Boris Karloff, Regis Toomey, Henry Kolker, Marie Wilson, Eddie Craven, Eddie Acuff. Contrary to regulations, a private in the US army brings his wife with him to the Government arsenal in Powder Island fortress, hidden in his kitbag. While endeavouring to hide her in a disused armoury, he comes upon the body of a man pinioned to the rafters with a bayonet and his wife's screams reveal them all to the guard. Colonel Hackett, advised of the crime, sends for Colonel Rogers of the Intelligence Department and meanwhile more startling events take place, which are all attributed to the murderer. Suspicion falls on Jevries (Boris Karloff) a civilian on the island, when Rogers, who appears prejudiced against him from the start, recounts the story of an earlier crime of vengeance, for which Jevries has been imprisoned and only lately released. But while Jevries is held under guard it falls to the lot of the young wife to discover the real culprit in a cleverly tense situation.

1938 *Mr Wong – Detective* Monogram Distribution: Pathe. Director: William Nigh. Story and screenplay by Houston Branch. Cert. 'A'. With Boris Karloff, Grant Withers, Dorothy Tree, Maxine Jennings, Evelyn Brent. Boris Karloff in the first of a new series as Mr Wong, the unassuming and meticulous specialist in crime investigation. Mr Wong is asked to help a large chemical firm to investigate murderous threats. As his investigations proceed three murders take place, the victims being the partners in the manufacture of poison gas. The police are at a loss to find the cause of death in each case and various suspects are held. Meanwhile Mr Wong works on patiently and finally solves the mystery.

1939 *Devil's Island* Warner Brothers Director: William Clemens. Screenplay by Kenneth Gamet and Don Ryan; from the original story by Anthony Caldeway and Raymond L Schrock. Not released in Britain. With Boris Karloff, Nedda Harrigan, James Stephenson, Adia Kuznetsoff, Rolla Gourvitch. A grim story of a French doctor, Dr Gaudet (Boris Karloff) who aids a wounded, escaped prisoner and is sentenced to Devil's Island for treason. After undergoing torture he escapes but is recaptured to find that the records of the prison's director, stolen by an accomplice of the physician, had earned him a pardon by virtue of the revelations of the peculations of the prison's head.

1939 *The Mystery of Mr Wong* Monogram Distribution: Pathe. Director: William Nigh. Cert 'U'. With Boris Karloff, Dorothy Tree, Grant Withers, Lotus Long, Morgan Wallace, Holmes Herbert, Craig Reynolds. Edwards, a collector of curios and precious stones, illegally gains possession of a famous gem, the 'Eye of the Moon', seized from the Nanking museum during a riot. He then receives a note stating that as possessor of the famous gem his life is in danger. He confides in Mr Wong showing him a letter to be opened in the event of his sudden death which will give Wong a clue to the identity of the killer. During a game of charades Edwards is shot dead and Wong discovers that the all-important letter has been stolen. Despite this, however, he eventually tracks down the murderer.

1939 *Mr Wong in Chinatown* Monogram Distribution: Pathe. Director: William Nigh. Cert. 'A'. Reissued, 1946. With Boris Karloff, Grant Withers, Marjorie Reynolds, William Royle. Princess Lin Haw, newly arrived in the United States, calls on

Detective James Lee Wong, but before he can learn the purpose of her visit she is killed by an unseen hand. With her last remaining strength she has scribbled on paper 'Captain J . . .' Aided by Inspector Street, Wong sets out to solve the mystery. Two men whose names begin with 'J' are suspected, but eventually Wong discovers the murderer to be a bank man with whom the princess has lodged a large sum of money, having been in the commission of the Chinese Government.

1939 *The Man They Could Not Hang* Columbia Director: Nick Grinde. Cert. 'H'. With Boris Karloff, Lorna Gray, Robert Wilcox, Roger Prior, Ann Doran, Don Beddoe. The story centres round the discovery of a mechanical 'heart' that restores life to the dead, but when it is actually tried out, the whole character of the revived man is changed and instead of being a benevolent doctor, he is a merciless killer seeking revenge on the judge and jury who wronged him. Having trapped them in an empty house he proceeds to kill them but is at length himself shot – and he dies for the second time.

1939 *Son of Frankenstein* Universal Director: Rowland V Lee. Distribution: General Films. Cert. 'H'. With Basil Rathbone, Boris Karloff, Bela Lugosi, Josephine Hutchinson, Lionel Atwill. The third of the Frankenstein films; this time Baron Wolf von Frankenstein returns to his father's castle from America to discover the monster in a coma under the care of a crazy shepherd. The monster is revived and after a series of murders, the Baron's son is seized by the monster, but, in the nick of time, is rescued as the monster hurtles backwards into a scalding sulphur pit.

1939 *Tower of London* Universal Director: Rowland V Lee. Distribution: General Films. Cert. 'A'. With Basil Rathbone, Boris Karloff, Nan Grey, Ian Hunter, Vincent Price, Barbara O'Neil. An excellent historical drama of the reign of Edward IV, Edward V and Richard III, with Boris Karloff as the grim clubfoot executioner, Mord.

1940 *Mr Wong at Headquarters* Monogram Director: William Nigh. Distribution: Pathe. International Cert. 'A'. (Entitled *The Fatal Hour* in USA.) With Boris Karloff, Grant Withers, Marjorie Reynolds, Charles Trowbridge. The fourth film featuring Boris Karloff as the criminal investigation specialist. This time he is called in by Captain Street whose best friend, Detective O'Grady, has been murdered. Karloff moved quietly through this film which was full of thrills and murders and eventually emerged unscathed from an apparently impossible situation to solve the mystery. Reissued, 1946.

1940 *Behind the Door* Columbia Director: Nick Grinde. Cert. 'A'. (Entitled *The Man with Nine Lives* in USA.) With Boris Karloff, Jo Ann Sayers, Roger Pryor, Stanley Brown, John Dilson, Hal Taliaferro. A medical mystery drama with a brilliant young scientist going in search of Dr Leon Kravaal (Boris Karloff), a pioneer in the method of curing cancer by freezing, who has disappeared ten years before. He finds Dr Kravaal, together with some other men, frozen and in a state of coma on a secret island. They are revived and in spite of the opposition which leads to the death of Dr Kravaal and his companions, the secret formula is discovered and, presumably, cancer is no longer a danger.

1940 *The Mystery of the 'Wentworth Castle'* Monogram Director: William Nigh. Cert. 'A'. (Entitled *Doomed to Die* in USA.) With Boris Karloff, Grant Withers, Marjorie Reynolds, William Stelling, Melvin Lang, Guy Usher. Adapted by Michael Jocoby from a story by Hugh Wiley. In this, the last of the Wong mysteries, the oriental criminologist solves the mysterious murder of a shipowner and clears an innocent young man of suspected murder. Reissued in 1947.

1940 *Enemy Agent* Warner Brothers Director: Terry Morse. Cert. 'A'. (Entitled *British Intelligence* in USA). With Boris Karloff, Margaret Lindsay, Maris Wrixon, Bruce Lester, Holmes Herbert, Leonard Mudie. This spy drama of the Great War, a remake of *Three Faces East*, had the British Secret Service hard put to it to discover the whereabouts and identity of the German ace-spy Strendler (Boris Karloff) who has managed to get a job as a butler in the home of a Cabinet Minister. To the house comes Helene, a British SS agent posing as a German spy, who is supposed to report to Strendler. A trap is set to catch Strendler by announcing that a secret meeting of the Cabinet will be held and Strendler sets a time bomb to go off during the meeting. Helene discovers this and is wounded by Strendler as she tries to save the situation. Although the British Intelligence arrives in time, Strendler escapes, but not for long, as he is killed almost at once in a German air-raid.

1940 *Black Friday* Universal Director: Arthur Lubin. Cert. 'A'. With Boris Karloff, Bela Lugosi, Stanley Ridges, Anne Nagel, Anne Gwynn. Karloff, an absent-minded professor of English literature, is accidentally run down in the street during a car battle between gangsters. He and one of the gang are taken to hospital where an eminent brain specialist and friend of Professor Kingsley, decides to save the latter's life by transplanting into his skull part of the gangster's brain. As a result the professor develops a dual personality, being at times himself and at others, the gangster. In New York, where he is taken in the hope of being able to discover the gangster's hidden hoard, he kills his gangster enemies and retrieves the stolen money. He then returns to his normal self and resumes teaching at the University. The sound of an ambulance siren, however, causes a reversion to the gangster influence and when he tries to kill the specialist's daughter, the specialist shoots him and goes to the electric chair, leaving his records of the case for humanity.

1940 *Before I Hang* Columbia Director: Nick Grinde. From a screenplay by Robert D. Andrews. Cert. 'A'. With Boris Karloff, Evelyn Keyes, Bruce Bennett, Pedro De Cordoba, Edward Van Sloan. Boris Karloff, as Dr John Garth, an elderly scientist, in attempting to prove that he has dis-covered a cure for death, kills and is sentenced to be hanged, but while awaiting execution he becomes friendly with the prison surgeon and the two men continue Garth's experiments in the prison laboratory.

1940 *You'll Find Out* RKO Radio Director: David Butler. Cert. 'A'. With Kay Kyser, Peter Lorre, Boris Karloff, Bela Lugosi, Helen Parrish. A comedy mystery-thriller, with music.

1941 *The Ape* Monogram Distribution: Pathe. Director: William Nigh. Cert. 'A'. With Boris Karloff, Maris Wrixon, Gertrude Hoffmann, Henry Hall, Gene O'Donnell. (Reissued 1947.) Boris Karloff plays the part of Dr Garth whose wife and child die of paralysis and he decides to dedicate his life to finding a cure for this malady. He thinks that a serum from the spinal column of a human being may be the answer and when the wounded trainer of a circus ape dies in his surgery, the doctor sees his opportunity and takes the liquid he needs. The serum works on a girl patient but more is needed for a complete cure. The ape breaks into Dr Garth's laboratory so he kills it and, using the skin as a disguise, sets out to get more liquid for the serum. He is eventually shot, but as he dies he sees his patient rise from her chair apparently cured.

1941 *The Devil Commands* Columbia Director: Edward Dmytryk. Screenplay by Robert D Andrews and Milton Gunzburg from the novel *Edge of Running Water* by William Stone. Cert. 'A'. With Boris Karloff, Anne Revere, Amanda Duff, Richard Fiske. A drama involving Dr Julian Blair (Boris Karloff) a highly respected scientist who has just perfected an apparatus for measuring brain impulses and has recorded those of his wife, when she is killed in a car smash. Half-demented with grief, he attempts to communicate with her spirit through the brain machine which he does with the help of a spiritualist medium. One of his assistants loses some of his faculties after an experiment and Blair and the medium are forced to go into hiding in a small northern town in England. There one day, the housekeeper, whose suspicions have been aroused, is killed while spying on the couple and the doctor accidentally kills the medium. At length the villagers storm the house, but the apparatus explodes and the doctor is killed.

1943 *The Bogie Man Will Get You* Columbia Director: Lew Landers, Cert. 'A'. With Boris Karloff, Peter Lorre, Maxie Rosenbloom, Larry Parks. A witless comedy-horror film obviously inspired by the success of *Arsenic and Old Lace*.

1944 *The Climax* Universal Distribution: General Films. Producer/Director: George Waggner. Based on the play by Edward Locke. Cert 'A'. With Susanna Foster, Turhan Bey, Boris Karloff, Gale Sondergaard, June Vincent, Jane Farror, Thomas Gomer. A technicolor drama with Boris Karloff as Dr Hohner.

1945 *The Body Snatchers* RKO Radio Director: Robert Wise. Produced by Val Lewton. From a screenplay by Philip MacDonald and Carlos Keith based on a novel by Robert Louis Stevenson. Cert. 'A'. With Boris Karloff, Bela Lugosi, Henry Daniel, Edith Atwater, Russel Wade. The story opens in Edinburgh in 1832 after a period of public agitation against the pest of grave-robbery. Among those who still carry on the grim trade is Grey, ostensibly a coach-driver. Formerly a medical student who has been convicted of the offence, he cherishes a lasting grudge against a one-time colleague, MacFarlane, who escaped detection. His threats of exposure force MacFarlane, now an eminent surgeon, to yeild to Grey's insistence on being employed to secure bodies for him, for large sums of money. The two are shadowed by MacFarlane's servant who, when he has collected sufficient evidence, calls on Grey for the purpose of blackmailing him. Grey murders him and carries his body to MacFarlane, who in turn kills his tormentor. Realising that he must now rely on his own efforts to obtain bodies needed for scientific purposes, MacFarlane steals the body of a woman from a newly-dug grave. Driving homewards through the night, MacFarlane imagines the dead body of the woman beside him to be that of his victim Grey, and pulling aside the wrappings, sees distinctly the face of Grey. His terrified screams cause the horses to bolt so that he is thrown from the carriage and killed.

1945 *The Isle of the Dead* RKO Radio Director: Mark Robson. Produced by Val Lewton. Screenplay by Ardel Wray and Josef Mischel. Cert. 'X'. With Boris Karloff, Ellen Drew, Marc Cramer, Katherine Emery, Helene Thimig. A mystery-drama set on a small burial island off the coast of Greece with Boris Karloff as a Greek general in the Balkan War visiting the island where his wife was buried fifteen years before. He is accompanied by an American newspaperman and they find the coffin empty and set off in search of the violators. They become guests of an archaeologist whose household is dominated by superstition. The general comes to believe that a beautiful girl is a vampire whose soul is evil and he endeavours to kill her for the good of the rest of the guests, moved to the island after a plague scare. After hair-raising incidents including a woman being entombed alive; another plunging to her death from a cliff and several gruesome murders, the newspaperman and the girl safely leave the island. This film was banned in England for over ten years.

1945 *House of Frankenstein* Universal Director: Erle C Kenton. Screenplay by Edward T Lowe based on an original story by Curt Siodmak. Cert. 'H'. With Boris Karloff, Lon Chaney Jnr, Anne Gwynne, Lionel Atwill, J Carroll Naish, John Carradine, George Zucco, Sig Rumann. Boris Karloff, as Dr Gustov Neumann, escapes from prison for his experiments in black magic.

1946 *Bedlam* RKO Radio Director: Mark Robson. Produced by Val Lewton. From a screenplay by Mark Robson and Carlos Keith. Photographer: Nicholas Musuraca. With Boris Karloff, Anna Lee, Billy House, Richard Fraser. The story of Karloff, as the head of the notorious insane asylum in 1773, obsequious to social superiors and cruel to his charges and Anna Lee, as the mistress of the wealthy man responsible for Karloff's position. When she turns against her nobleman and attempts to bring about reforms in the treatment of the insane, Karloff manages to get her committed to the asylum, where she achieves some improvement of conditions before escaping and bringing official intervention. ('An elaborate improvisation, but not an improvement, on one of Hogarth's drawings.') Not released in Britain.

1946 *The Man Who Dared* Columbia Director: John Sturges. Cert. 'A'. With Boris Karloff, George Macready, Leslie Brooks. A newspaper columnist who was once responsible for the conviction of an innocent man on circumstantial evidence, allows himself to be convicted for murder, on circumstantial evidence alone, so that he can prove its insufficiency. Unfortunately, his friend who has the proof of his innocence which is to be produced at the appropriate moment, is robbed and severely injured by the real murderer, played by Boris Karloff; however, the newspaper man manages to escape from prison and surmounts dangers and difficulties before proving his innocence and the truth of his story.

1947 *Personal Column* Hunt Stromberg (Released through United Artists.) Director: Douglas Sirk. Screenplay by Leo Rosten. Produced by James Nasser. Cert. 'A'. (Entitled *Lured* in USA.) Reissued, 1955. With George Sanders, Charles Coburn, Lucille Ball, Boris Karloff, Alan Mowbray, Sir Cedric Hardwicke, George Zucco. The story of a homicidal maniac who makes a speciality of killing young girls whom he contacts through the Personal Column of newspapers; Karloff playing a crazed clothes designer.

1947 *The Secret Life of Walter Mitty* RKO Radio Director: Norman Z McLeod. Cert 'U'. With Danny Kaye, Virginia Mayo, Boris Karloff, Fay Bainter, Ann Rutherford, Thurston Hall. A comedy in colour with Danny Kaye as Walter Mitty who escapes from his humdrum existence by dreaming of himself as the hero of various romantic situations always involving the same girl. These become complicated when he meets her in reality and is called upon to act his heroic daydreams. Boris Karloff is the leader of a jewel-thief gang.

1947 *Dick Tracy's Amazing Adventure* RKO Radio Director: John Rawlins. Cert. 'A'. (Entitled *Dick Tracy Meets Gruesome* in USA). With Boris Karloff, Ralph Byrd, Anne Gwynne. Dick Tracy, of American comic-strip fame, meets up with Boris Karloff, as Gruesome, an ex-convict who is working a bank robbery scheme. A couple of murders, a hair-raising car chase and finally Tracy, single-handed, apprehends Gruesome.

1947 *Unconquered* Paramount Produced and Directed by Cecil B de Mille. Cert. 'A'. With Paulette Goddard, Gary Cooper, Howard Da Silva, Boris Karloff, Cecil Kellaway, Ward Bond, Henry Wilcoxon. A technicolor spectacular telling the story of America's colonial struggle for the empire of the Indians in 1763 – with Boris Karloff as Guyasuta, Chief of the Senecas; a long-haired Indian.

1948 *Tap Roots* Universal-International Distribution: General Films. Director: George Marshall. Cert. 'A'. With Van Heflin, Susan Hayward, Boris

Karloff, Julie London, Ward Bond, Whitfield Connor, Richard Long. A technicolor saga of the American Civil War dealing with the Dabney family of Lebanon County who decide to remain neutral when Mississipi withdraws from the Union. The head of the family defends his neutrality by force and, because he is in love with a Dabney daughter, Keith Alex, a local newspaperman, supports him. Despite sacrifices the Dabney cause inevitably fails and the young couple decide to stay and rebuild in Lebanon County. There are a number of spirited battles and Boris Karloff appears as Tishomingo, a friendly and educated Choctaw Indian.

1949 *Abbott and Costello Meet the Killer, Boris Karloff* Universal-International   Director: Charles T Barton. Cert. 'A'. With Bud Abbot, Lou Costello, Boris Karloff, Lenore Aubert, Gar Moore, Alan Mowbray. A comedy thriller written by Hugh Wedlock Jnr. Strange occurrences at the Lost Cavens Hotel culminate in murder and the bellboy is in danger from both the police and the real murderers. Karloff was a phony spiritualist.

1949 *The Emperor's Nightingale* Rembrandt Films Produced by William L Snyder. Colour by Agfacolour. A Czech puppet film based on a tale by Hans Christian Andersen. Narration by Boris Karloff.

1951 *The Strange Door* Universal-International Director: Joseph Pevney. Script by Jerry Sackheim, based on Robert Louis Stevenson's *The Sire de Maletroit's Door*. Cert. 'A'. With Charles Laughton, Boris Karloff, Sally Forrest, Richard Stapley, Michael

Pate, Paul Cavanagh. An influential citizen of
eighteenth century France, Alan Sire de Maletroit
(Charles Laughton) is a cruel tyrant given to fits
of insanity resulting from his childhood sweetheart's marriage to his brother twenty years
before. The woman died giving birth to a daughter
in the second year of her marriage and the brother
has been presumed dead too, but he has been
kept a prisoner by Alan throughout the ensuing
years in a dungeon in the Maletroit chateau.
Their daughter Blanche (Sally Forrest) lives with
her uncle, unaware that her father is imprisoned
in the same building, and resigned to the fact her
uncle plans to marry her off to a man of his own
choice. Crazed with thoughts of revenge, Alan has
long awaited Blanche's coming-of-age so that he
can search out 'the worst rogue in France' and join
them in matrimony. He selects Denis de Beaulieu,
a heavy-drinking, wastrel scion of a famous French
family. Denis is lured to the chateau and thrown
into a dungeon until he will agree to marry
Blanche. Contrary to Alan's plans, however, the
two young people fall in love. When Alan tries to
prevent their escape he is thwarted by Voltan
(Boris Karloff), his half-witted servant, who saves
the two lovers from death.

1952 *The Black Castle* Universal-International Distribu-
tion: General Film Distributors. Director: Nathan
Juran. Story and screenplay by Jerry Sackheim.
Cert. 'A'. With Richard Greene, Stephen
MacNally, Boris Karloff, Paula Corday, Lon
Chaney. The castle, replete with hungry alligator

pool, secret passages and torture chambers, is the headquarters of a sinister Austrian Count who plots hideous deaths for his enemies. A young adventurer believes his two friends were killed by the Count and gaining admittance to the castle, he fights against all intrigues and protects the Count's unwilling bride with the help of an enslaved doctor (Karloff).

1953 *Abbott and Costello Meet Dr Jekyll and Mr Hyde* Universal-International Distribution: General Film Distributors. Director: Charles Lamont. Cert. 'X'. Based on stories by Sidney Fields and Grant Garrett from a screenplay by Leo Loeb and John Grant. With Bud Abbot, Lou Costello, Boris Karloff, Helen Westcott, Craig Stevens, Reginald Denny. London at the turn of the century is terrorised by the murders committed by an unknown monster who is in fact Dr Jekyll *alter ego* Mr Hyde (Boris Karloff). Jekyll, jealous of the love of Bruce Adams, a newspaper reporter, for his suffragette ward, Vicky Edwards, determines to murder Bruce, in the person of Mr Hyde. Tubby and Slim, American detectives, attached to Scotland Yard, are unable to convince anyone of the truth of their discovery: that Jekyll periodically turns into Hyde, until at last Tubby, too, is accidentally converted into a monster. Rival monsters are chased across London and Jekyll commits suicide while Tubby is taken to the police station. Before returning to his normal self he bites the policemen there with the result that they all turn into monsters!

1953 *Colonel March Investigates* Criterion Film Productions Director: Cyril Endfield. Distribution: Eros. Cert. 'A'. With Boris Karloff, Joan Sims, Dana Wynter. Three stories featuring the head of the Department of Queer Complaints at Scotland Yard who brings the three miscreants to justice.

1953 *Il Mostro dell'Isola* (*The Monster of the Island*) Romana Films (Italy) Director: Roberto Montero. With Renato Vicario, Franca Marzi, Jole Fierro. Karloff was a ferocious head of a band of dope-smugglers on the island of Ischia.

1953 *Sabaka* Director: Frank Ferrin. Production: Frank Ferrin Company. Distribution: United Artists. Cert. 'U'. (Entitled *The Hindu* in USA.) Filmed in colour in India with Boris Karloff, Nino Marcel, Lou Krugman, Reginald Denny, Victor Jory, this is the story of a young Mahout who loses his sister and brother in a forest fire, started by a high priestess of the worshippers of Sabaka, the Fire Demon; and of his efforts at vengeance by taking the law into his own hands. When he, in turn, is captured after he has discovered the secret hide-out of the devil worshippers, he is rescued by his pet elephant and tiger. Karloff was the local rajah's military chief.

1956 *Voodoo Island* Bel Air Productions Distribution: United Artists. Director: Reginald Le Borg. Cert. 'A'. With Boris Karloff, Beverly Tyler, Murvyn Vye, Elisha Cook. Karloff, almost without make-up, is a debunker of superstitions who leads an expedition to a tropical island where mysterious things occur; when members of the party are devoured by carnivorous plants and others become zombies, Karloff begins to believe in voodoo.

1957 *The Juggler of Our Lady* 20th-Century Fox Director: Paul Terry. An Italian-made techni-color cartoon in cinemascope with commentary by Boris Karloff.

1958 *Frankenstein 1970* Bel Air Productions Distribu-tion: Associated British-Pathe. Director: Howard W Koch. From a story by Aubrey Schenck and Charles A Moss. Cert. 'X'. Filmed in Cinemascope, with Boris Karloff, Tom Duggan, Jana Lund, Donald Barry, Charlotte Austin. Baron Victor von Frankenstein, great-grandson of the original creator of the monster and the last of his line (Boris Karloff) permits a television film unit to use his castle to film a series celebrating the 150th-anniversary of the creation of the monster in order to obtain money to further his efforts to bring his own monster to life. The monster disposes of several of the unit, and others, before it and its creator are destroyed in atomic steam.

1958 *Grip of the Strangler* MGM Distribution: Eros. Director: Robert Day. Cert. 'X'. (Entitled *The Haunted Strangler* in USA.) Filmed in England, with Boris Karloff, Jean Kent, Elizabeth Allen, Tim Turner, Anthony Dawson, Diane Aubrey. A New-gate prison public execution is followed by further macabre events involving an investigating novelist. The trail ends at the grave of the executed man. Karloff is the novelist investigating the gruesome twenty-year-old crime which, it turns out, he had himself committed in a secondary personality.

1962 *Corridors of Blood* MGM Director: Robert Day. Cert. 'X'. Filmed in Britain, with Boris Karloff, Betta St John, Adrienne Corri, Christopher Lee, Finlay Currie, Francis De Wolff. Costume horror melodrama about body snatchers and anaesthesia. Karloff was a doctor in the early days of anaesthetics, who falls into the clutches of thieves and murderers.

1962 *The Raven* American-International Producer/ Director: Roger Corman. Panavision/Pathecolour. Cert. 'X'. With Vincent Price, Peter Lorre, Boris Karloff, Hazel Court, Olive Sturgess, Jack Nicholson, William Baskin. 'A spoof on every horror film', this travesty of Edgar Allan Poe's masterpiece is a light-hearted and occasionally funny tale with Karloff as a wicked wizard who lived in a slimy green castle, in conflict with another sorcerer – Vincent Price. The prologue of Vincent Price reading Poe's poem *The Raven* was enjoyable.

1963 *The Terror* American-International Producer/ Director: Roger Corman. Filmed in Vistascope/ Pathecolour. Cert. 'X'. With Boris Karloff, Jack Nicholson, Sandra Knight, Richard Miller Dorothy Neumann, Jonathan Haze. Karloff, as a necrophilic baron intent on preserving his dead wife, comes to grips with Nicholson, who attempts to rescue her, but when they leave the evil castle together she disintegrates in his arms.

1963 *The Comedy of Terrors* American-International Director: Roger Corman. Filmed in Cinemascope and Eastmancolour by Pathe. Cert. 'X'. With Vincent Price, Peter Lorre, Boris Karloff, Basil

Rathbone, Joe E Brown, Joyce Jamieson. Vincent Price and Peter Lorre, two New England undertakers, find business slack and decide to go out and make their own employment. Karloff had a minor role as Price's senile father-in-law, Amos Hinchley.

1963 *Black Sabbath* (*I Tre Volti della Paura*) Emmepi/ Galatea/Lyre American-International Director: Mario Bara. Screenplay by Marcello Fondato. Photography by Ubaldo Terzano. Music: Les Baxter. Cert. 'X'. With Boris Karloff, Susy Anderson, Mark Damon, Michele Mercier, Lidia Alfonsi, Jacqueline Pierreux, Milly Monti. An Italian-made three-part colour demonthology. *The Drop of Water* from a story by Chekov concerns a nurse who steals a jewel from a corpse and is haunted by 'a drop of water'. In *The Telephone*, from a story by F G Snyder, a girl receives a telephone call from a boy friend she sent to the gallows; he revisits her and she stabs him to death but a second later the telephone rings again and the voice of the dead man tells her: 'Don't worry, darling, you can never kill me . . .' *The Wrudalak* is the longest and most frightening story of the three and the only one in which Boris Karloff appears. He is an East European vampire who carries with him someone's head in a sack; one night he tears out the throat of his four-year-old grandson . . . Adapted from a Tolstoi story. Karloff did his own English dubbing and linked the stories in exactly the right key.

1964 *Bikini Beach* American-International Director:

William Asher. Filmed in Panavision and Technicolor. Not released in Britain. Karloff had a guest appearance only.

1964 *Today's Teen* 20th-Century Fox A short, with Karloff as narrator.

1965 *Monster of Terror* Anglo-American (Released through Warner-Pathe.) Director: Daniel Haller. Producer: Pat Green. Colour by Colorscope. Screenplay by Jerry Sohl from *Colour Out of Space* by H P Lovecraft. (Entitled *Die, Monster, Die* in USA.) With Karloff, Nick Adams, Suzan Farmer, Freda Jackson, Terence De Marney, Patrick Magee, Leslie Dwyer, Paul Farrel. Perhaps the first truly contemporary terror story with science-fiction threats from outer space together with classic, Gothic terror ingredients. Karloff sets out an ordinary, kindly man and ends up a hideous monster.

1966 *The Daydreamer* Embassy Director: Jules Bass. A full-length animagic feature with Karloff's voice for *The Rat*.

1966 *The Venetian Affair* Jerry Thorpe Production. Presented by MGM. Director: Jerry Thorpe. Script by E Jack Neuman. Based on a best-selling novel by Helen McInnes. Music by Lalo Schifrin. Filmed in Metrocolor Panavision. Cert. 'A'. With Robert Vaughan, Elke Sommer, Karl Boehm, Boris Karloff. When an American diplomat blows up a peace conference, killing all the delegates including himself, during a session in Venice, consternation is widespread. Robert Vaughan is a syndicated reporter-photographer who is rushed from New York. Karloff (Dr Pierre Vaugiroud) is a political scientist who has a secret report on the affair. He maintains that the explosion was executed only to create political distrust among nations and insists on revealing the terrible secret of how a man was induced to do the deed. It is later realised that the old man is drugged and Karloff is just stopped as he is about to repeat the horrible event which set all this in motion. Beautiful Venetian location photography. *The Times* commented: 'a really fast, tough, old-fashioned detective thriller, with plenty of enjoyable incomprehensible complexity and no time for anyone to stop and ask awkward questions.'

1967 *El Coleccionista de Cadaveres*(*The Corpse Collector*) Hispamer Films Director: Santos Alcocer. Karloff played a blind sculptor and the film was shown in America under the title *Blind Man's Bluff*. It was released in Britain in 1971 under the title *Cauldron of Blood*.

1967 *Ghost in the Invisible Bikini* American-International Director: Don Weis. With Boris Karloff, Tommy Kirk, Deborah Walley, Aron Kincaid, Jesse White, Harvey Lennbeck, Nancy Sinatra, Francis X Bushman, Basil Rathbone, Susan Hart. Not released in Britain.

1967 *Mad Monster Party* Embassy Director: Jules Bass. A full-length animagic feature with Karloff doing the voice-over for the Monster.

1967 *The Sorcerers* British Tigon/Curtwel/Global Director: Michael Reeves. Eastmancolour. From a screenplay by Michael Reeves and Tom Baker. Produced by Patrick Curtis and Tony Tenser.

Cert. 'X'. With Boris Karloff, Catherine Lacy, Ian Oglivy, Elizabeth Ercy, Victor Henry, Susan George. An ageing scientist and his wife devise a machine with which they find they can inhabit the mind of another person, control him and experience his sensations. They take over the mind of a young man who kills two young girls and beats up his friend. Finally the professor (Boris Karloff) causes the young man's car to crash, and as the flames take hold the professor and his wife die in flames simultaneously. As one critic said: 'To watch Boris Karloff, bearded and limping, re-enact the role of a mad scientist, is to watch one of the legends of the cinema at work. And he does not disappoint.'

1967 *Mondo Balordo* Cineproduzioni-Ivanhoe Director: Roberto Bianchi Montero. Karloff was the narrator.

1968 *The Witch House* Director: Michael Reed. Not released in Britain.

1968 *Curse of the Crimson Altar* Tigon British/American-International Director: Vernon Sewell. Executive Producer: Tony Tenser. Producer: Louis M Heyward. Script by Mervyn Haisman and Henry Lincoln with additional material by Gerry Levy. Photography: Johnny Coquillon. Eastman Colour. Music: Peter Knight. Cert. 'X'. With Boris Karloff, Christopher Lee, Mark Eden, Virginia Wetherell, Barbara Steele, Rupert Davies, Michael Gough, Rosemarie Reede, Derek Tansley, Michele Warren, Ron Pember, Denys Peek, Nita Lorraine, Carol Anne, Jenny Shaw, Vivienne Carlton.

Robert Manning (Mark Eden) visits Craxted Lodge on account of the disappearance of his brother Peter (Denys Peek), arriving on the eve of a village festivity celebrating the burning of Lavinia, the village witch, three hundred years before. At the Lodge its owner J D Morley, (Christopher Lee) denies all knowledge of Peter but Robert Manning discovers that the Manning family originally came from the village and unearths evidence that his brother did in fact stay at the Lodge. He is then told that his brother is dead. On two successive nights he has a vivid dream in which he is summoned by his brother to a mysterious chamber where Lavinia (Barbara Steele), the notorious witch, tries to force him to sign a confession amid the paraphernalia of black magic. On the second occasion he wakes to find his arm bleeding profusely. He then discovers a secret passage leading from his room to the mysterious chamber and finds the body of the butler (Michael Gough). Trapped by Morley who has sworn to avenge his ancestor Lavinia by eliminating the descendants of her accusers, he prepares to kill Robert and Eve (Virginia Wetherall), Morley's neice, when they are saved by witchcraft expert Professor Marsh (Boris Karloff). Morley sets fire to the Lodge and dies in the flames, transformed into Lavinia. A disappointing film with a 'deliciously bilious opening' (*Monthly Film Bulletin*), and a very mild 'wild' party, but otherwise one of the tamest horror films for a long time. Even the ground fog swirling round the gnarled trees; twigs that crumble into dust at the merest touch and desolation beautifully conceived, could not make up for the mediocre quality of the whole film.

1969 *Targets* Paramount Produced and Directed by Peter Bogdanovich. Screenplay by Peter Bogdanovich. Story by Polly Platt and Peter Bogdanovich. Director of Photography: Laszlo Kovacs. Cert. 'X'. (Entitled *Before I Die* in USA.) With Boris Karloff, Tim O'Kelly, Nancy Hsueh, James Brown, Sandy Baron, Arthur Peterson, Mary Jackson, Tanya Morgan, Monty Landis. Byron Orlok (Boris Karloff) is a popular actor, famous for his horror roles, who is growing old and decides to retire. 'Today's world,' he says, 'belongs to the young.' Bobby Thompson (Tim O'Kelly) is a young married man with an obsession for guns. From inside a gunshop he focuses the crosshairs of a telescopic rifle on Byron Orlok as he passes. Thompson buys the gun and adds it to the pistols, revolvers, rifles, knives and bullets in the boot of his car. That night, after quarrelling with his producer and his secretary (Nancy Hsueh), Byron Orlok drinks half a bottle of whiskey and watches one of his old films on television (*The Criminal Code*). Sam (played by Peter Bogdanovich), a young director-writer who hoped Orlok would make a new film with him, arrives and the old man tries to explain his reason for quitting. He feels that he has become a joke: his kind of horror is 'high camp' today; newspaper headlines about inexplicable violence are more horrible than anything he could

act in. Next morning real horror begins when
Bobby Thompson has a breakdown and, just
before noon, shoots his wife, his mother and a boy
delivering groceries. He orders 300 rounds of
ammunition at a local gunshop and drives out to a
group of gas tanks overlooking a motorway.
Here he climbs to a vantage point and aims at
passing cars. He shoots and hits a woman in a
station wagon, misses a young couple in a con-
vertible and hits an elderly man in the back seat
of a sports car. He hits the driver of another car
which swerves on to the side of the road and stops.
A woman gets out, tries to open the driver's door,
then decides to stop another car for help. As she
runs away Thompson shoots her in the back. A
gas tank worker hears the shooting and climbs to
investigate: he too is killed. As police begin to
arrive Thompson escapes, speeds through a red
light and turns into a drive-in cinema which is
showing Byron Orlok's latest film (*The Terror*),
and where the star has agreed to make a farewell
personal appearance. Thompson climbs the screen
tower and picks off people in their cars with his
rifle. The carnage grows and panic breaks out as
Byron Orlok arrives. He walks towards the gun-
man who finds himself confronting two Byron
Orloks, one on the screen and the other advancing
towards him, an aged but determined man with
a walking stick . . .

The film was memorable on many counts, not
least because of first-rate use of natural sound and
complete absence of background or mood music
'The most important and surprising film of the

week,' said Michael Billington in *The Illustrated London News;* 'Bogdanovich has an instinct for film . . . more will obviously be heard of him.' Derek Malcolm in *The Guardian* suggested that Bogdanovich secured for Karloff perhaps his most moving performance – 'the more you think about *Targets,* the more it grows.' Originally running for ninety-two minutes, the British release was cut by twelve minutes. Karloff's rendering of *Appointment in Samarra* was especially enjoyable and, for once away from horror, he played quite straight and, as *The Times* said, the film 'must have come as a great pleasure and relief to him.' They summed up by saying: 'A distinguished directional debut and a movingly appropriate farewell to a great star.'

Credits and Acknowledgements
Miss Alice Roe; Mr Samuel Grafton; Cinema International Corporation; Universal Pictures; MGM – EMI Distributors Ltd; The Rank Organisation Ltd; United Artists Corporation Ltd; 20th-Century Pictures; Syndication International; Columbia Pictures; Julius Hagan Productions; Warner Brothers Pictures; Stratford Films Ltd; Philips Records Ltd; Tony Tenser Films Ltd; American International Pictures.

Index

229

INDEX

237